Valeria Sterzi
Deconstructing Gender in Carnival

POSTCOLONIAL STUDIES | Volume 7

Valeria Sterzi (Dr. phil.) received her PhD in Sociology at the University of Hamburg, Germany. Her research interests lie in the field of postcolonial and gender studies, including theories of identity, hybridity and multiculturalism, in the context of cultural productions, ritual theory, and performance practices.

Valeria Sterzi
Deconstructing Gender in Carnival
A Cross Cultural Investigation of a Social Ritual

[transcript]

Bibliographic information published by
the Deutsche Nationalbibliothek
The Deutsche Nationalbibliothek lists this publication in the Deutsche Nationalbibliografie; detailed bibliographic data are available in the Internet at http://dnb.d-nb.de

© 2010 transcript Verlag, Bielefeld

All rights reserved. No part of this book may be reprinted or reproduced or utilized in any form or by any electronic, mechanical, or other means, now known or hereafter invented, including photocopying and recording, or in any information storage or retrieval system, without permission in writing from the publisher.

Cover layout: Kordula Röckenhaus, Bielefeld
Cover illustration: © Valeria Sterzi
Proofread & typeset by Valeria Sterzi
Printed by Majuskel Medienproduktion GmbH, Wetzlar
ISBN 978-3-8376-1348-3

Distributed in North America by:

Transaction Publishers
New Brunswick (U.S.A.) and London (U.K.)

Transaction Publishers	Tel.: (732) 445-2280
Rutgers University	Fax: (732) 445-3138
35 Berrue Circle	for orders (U.S. only):
Piscataway, NJ 08854	toll free 888-999-6778

Contents

Introduction — 7

I. Definition of Post-Colonialism: Hybridity, Mimicry and National Identity — 23

II. Re-Inventing Culture: the Caribbean Example. Introducing the Caribbean: History and Society — 41

III. Gender and Post-Colonialism — 55
Pandora's Daughters: Origins of Women's Subordination — 55
   A Double Colonization — 64
From Another Point of View: Women of the Caribbean — 71

IV. Between Rite and Performance — 85
Religion and Society: From Rite to Performance and Social Change — 85

V. The World Upside-Down — 111
Theorizing Carnival: the Grotesque Realism of a Social Ritual — 111

VI. The Ambivalence of Trinidad Carnival. Music, Masking and Performance: the »Magical Mirror« of a Hybrid Society — 123
»All o' we is one«: Carnival as a Symbol of National Identity and Unity — 123
Carnival in Transition: Unmasking on the Street, Masking on the Stage. Dynamics and Contradictions of Women's Participation in Carnival — 151

VII. Conclusion — 179

References 185

Illustrations 201

INTRODUCTION

> »Hegel remarks somewhere[*] that all great world-historic facts and personages appear, so to speak, twice. He forgot to add: the first time as tragedy, the second time as farce.«[1]
> (Karl Marx, The Eighteenth Brumaire of Louis Bonaparte)

The Caribbean archipelago is characterized by diversity, in which colonial and post-colonial ideas have combined with West African, East Indian, Amerindian, and other non-western cultural traditions and legacies, creating together a variety of economical, political and cultural arrangements and praxis that define Caribbean societies.

Creole society is one way in which the region is captured to signify the blending of ethnicities, cultures, religions and languages, standing today as the global metaphor for notions of *diaspora*, *creolization*, religious syncretism, *hybridity*, cultural pluralism and *transnationality*, for both Caribbean identity and sense of belonging have been forged through a particular history and shaped by continual *interculturation*, *transculturation*, and negotiations between various socio-cultural groupings. Thus, more than just a geographical expression, the Caribbean defies static definitions.

Caribbean history is rich with tumultuous and cruel battles of conquest, forced migrations and endured labour, blended cultures, ethnic and natural diversity. Throughout its past, the Caribbean has revealed a great complexity of social relations and the influence of such variables as race, ethnicity, migration and multifaceted dependency (socio-economic condition, popular culture, institutional mimicry) on politics. Consequently, we

---

1 In Tucker, Robert, C. (1978): »The Marx-Engel Reader«, W.W Norton & Company, Princeton University, p. 595

might agree that Caribbean culture is the result of a syncretism that comes from the relationship among several human groups of different origins and from various types of cultural creativity, for the Caribbean islands have been and are still settings in which peoples of very different pasts, but fairly similar presents, jostled together in new sceneries with cultural accompaniments of heterogeneity and diversity as consequences.

Although there is a shared past behind the West Indies concerning diverse social, geographical, economical and historical aspects, the history, culture and social composition of each island is dissimilar. In fact, European conquest, slavery, the plantation economy, and the immigration had a different background and effect in each island. Thus West Indian performances, languages, social assumptions, music, etc have been influenced by diverse contexts, and therefore there is a past and present identity needing to be told through many different perspectives and voices.

If, according to Homi Bhabha, all cultures are intercultural and transnational and participate in an ongoing exchange with others, with elite and popular forms, in the process of creating and revitalizing their own identity according to their time, place, actualities, desires, and needs (Bhabha 1994), we may then say that the creative and imaginative vitality of the West Indies derives mainly from its different genes, cultures, histories and problems. Indeed, for a better and deeper understanding of political and cultural realities of the former British colonies in the Caribbean area, it is of primary importance to consider the British colonial practice of »divide and rule« as relevant in promoting class and racial divisions within the subordinate populations, and in yielding the consequences that in the post-independent Caribbean, have become manifested in the region's political culture. Race, class and gender inequalities, that were so crucial to the stability and effectiveness of colonial rule have mutated into the contemporary period and, although the colonizers are no longer present, the political consciousness of the wider population continues to be raced and classed.

Caribbean political culture had always been mirroring (and it still does) this debate over race, class, and gender, albeit under changed circumstances. In fact, if we agree that the history of Europe for the past few centuries had been profoundly shaped by the colonial interests , then there is a logic, in which much of the cultural expressions produced during that time can be said to be colonial, or, vice versa and as a consequence, postcolonial, even if only tangentially so.

Culture offers one of the most important ways in which these »new« perceptions are expressed, and it is through the various languages of culture such as literature, painting, sculpture, music and dance, that the day to day realities experienced by the colonised have been most powerfully encoded and so profoundly influential. Ideology does not concern just the political sphere, but it is related to all our mental structures, our beliefs, the concepts and the ways of expressing our relationships with the outside world.

The stratification of a society in classes, the subsistence of a superior race (of course white and belonging to the western world) and of an inferior (black/not European) the binary opposition of the humanity in »Us« as the representative of civilization and »Other« as primitive and uncivilized, are actually the result of complicated and lengthy cultural elaborations, shaped by the necessity of giving convincing motivations that legitimated the abuse of power and the political, cultural and economical dominion of one population over another.

Science, literature and other forms of art had the task to sponsor the empire policy by divulging its ideology, providing, at the same time, valid excuses. Cultural representations were central first to the process of colonizing other lands, and then again to the process of obtaining independence from the coloniser (the master), principally by deconstructing and subverting the canonical assumptions of culture imposed by the colonizers. Culture, in fact, has the political capacity of dismantling the hegemonic boundaries and the determinants that create unequal relations of power based on binary oppositions such as »us and them«, »first world and third world«, »white and black«, »coloniser and colonised«, »man and woman«.

The central strategy in transforming the imperialistic culture is the seizing of the self representation; the underlying of all economic, political and social resistance in the struggle over representation (that is, the process of giving a concrete form to ideological concepts) that occurs in language, writing and other forms of cultural productions and performances like carnival and theatre. The process of transformation- in which the continuous negotiation between the local and the global takes place- and the emerging shifting identities and realities create identity spaces by which the material and ideological dimension are deconstructed, and from which culturally specific - institutional/representational forms are produced.

The importance of cultural representations is referred to the process by which meanings are produced, and the ways in which images and texts reconstruct an ideological reality, rather than reflect the original sources they represent. When races, classes, sexes, and nations are viewed as distinct cultural constructions, performed in determinate relations within distinct structures, then the questions of cause, effect, and intervention can be posed within a new problematic, where inequality is social and contingent, not natural and necessary.

If cultural expressions are to consider the medium through which a given society is able to represent its common identity and communicate its contents, then, in various permutations and combinations, cultural developments have a revolutionary impact on different disciplines, which consequently cannot be considered in isolation from the growth of certain political movement such as feminism or anti-colonial struggles, mainly for the reason that both women and colonised peoples functioned in economies which depended on their labour, and both were subject to ideologies which justified this exploitation.

Therefore, in Chapter One I introduce the main debates over Post-Colonialism, Hybridity, and Mimicry. Nowadays a great number of scholars suggest that it would be more constructive to think about Post-Colonialism not just as something that comes after colonialism, or that signifies its cessation, but, in a flexible way, as the contestation of the colonial dominium and legacy.

In this regard, it was never conceived of as a grand theory, but as a methodology: first, for analysing the many strategies by which colonised people have engaged imperial discourse; and second, in order to study the ways in which many of those strategies are shared by former colonised societies that re-emerge in very different political and cultural circumstances. Thus, Post-Colonialism has often been concerned with the ways and extents to which culture and its representations are crucial to an identity formation and the construction of subjectivity. Consequently, according to Homi Bhabha:

»The colonial mimicry is the desire for a reformed, recognizable Other, as a subject of a difference that is almost the same, but not quite. Which is to say that the discourse of mimicry is constructed around an ambivalence; in order to be effective, mimicry must continually produce its slippage, its excess, its difference.«[2]

The great peculiarity of postcolonial phenomena consists in its capacity of transforming and »personalizing« expressions of different cultures into a definition of an own culture, that is, into a new own representation of the »Self« and the »Other«, emphasising how hybridity and the power it releases may allow a denotation of the replication of binary categories of the past and develop new anti-monolithic models of cultural exchange and growth.

Caribbean society, due to its particular history, has been and still is the protagonist of a continuous process of hybridization, which, because of its nature, is the source of phenomena that from different perspectives are simultaneously cross cultural and typical Caribbean. The peculiarity of its past, which had indelible consequences on the social, cultural, economic and political configuration of the region, still weighs on the present situation of each island. Thus, in Chapter Two I decided to make a brief and general excursus on the colonial history of the Caribbean, moving my interests on the past and contemporary diverse realities of Trinidad, to the Mecca of Carnival.

The contemporary Trinidad, less a melting pot than a mélange, remains a complex, fascinating fusion of race, ethnicity, class, culture and the inescapable legacies of slavery and the plantation system have enormously complicated the social stratification and the gender relations within the twin nation's reality. In fact, in almost every island, different gradations coexist and interpenetrate and each aspect of the Caribbean reveals blending and separatism side by side.

---

2   Bhabha, Homi, K. (1994): »The Location of Culture«, Routledge, New York and London, p. 86

The historical social processes and constructions that created social difference in terms of phenotype, ethnicity and gender in the Caribbean continue to shape and inform social relations in the twenty-first century, despite the lack of single, homogeneous, region-wide discourse on the subject, and in spite of the often-heard claims that racism no longer exists in the region. Therefore, Trinidad should be considered as a plural society, where a multitude of cultures and traditions interweave to form a »universal« continuum built up by unbroken intersections in which the habits of the various communities have intervened, in order to »invent« and create a national culture, in which, according to Sidney Mintz: »the cultural homogeneity of society (as it existed before western contact) is replaced by a culturally and racially heterogeneous society.«[3]

The former British colony has been studied for several decades and considered as an emblematic example of plural society, where Africans, Indians, East Indian, Europeans, Chinese and in a smaller number other kinds of ethnic groups cohabit the twin nation of Trinidad and Tobago. Despite the island achieved its freedom in 1962, becoming with Tobago the independent and formally unified nation of Trinidad and Tobago, race and class hierarchies, ethnic tension and fragmentation within the population are still realities which the Trinbagonians have to face.

In Trinidad, the process of nation building was complex and ambivalent, for it responded to the needs both of contrasting the imposed society structure and division, and of creating a new nation to which the different ethnic groups equally belonged and could be identified. If, according to Benedict Anderson (Anderson 1983), the nation is imagined, mythicized, precisely, is narrated via allusive and symbolic figures, then territory and culture can endow people with myths and symbols of unique identity; and cultural phenomena remain the dominant social bond par excellence.

---

3   Mintz, Sidney, W.: »Social Stratification and Cultural Pluralism«, in Horowitz, Michael M.(edited by) (1971): »Peoples and culture of the Caribbean, An Anthropological Reader«, The Natural History Press, Garden City, New York, p. 97

Throughout the XX century, the pursuit of the new Caribbean middle class was to create a pure Caribbean black identity which could symbolically bind the diverse ethnic groups, by constructing an ideal and utopian imagined community based on the myth of racial democracy. As a direct expression of the folk and, in a true sense, belonging to the black lower class, Carnival reflected all these expectations, becoming instrumentally constitutive of the shared imaginary sponsored by the new dominant culture.

Culture is depicted in terms of »shared values« and as the site of a common consensus, in which norms and values are deeply embedded. The analysis of culture with its diverse aspects has a great importance for its function of allowing links to be made between organizational process and individual identity, enabling us to explore the complexity of identity and the factors which influence the patterns of differentiation within an organization.

In the West Indies, men and women have been deeply socialized into certain sex-roles and attitudes, for gender categories are social constructions with a cultural specificity, thereby are sustained by a system of symbols, meanings, ascriptions and expectations. Therefore, I analyse the reasons and the mechanisms regulating the asymmetric relations of power actuated in different spheres (material and ideological) and the dynamic and interactive nature of socio/cultural and economic/political processes on a global (worldwide) and regional (Caribbean) scale.

Finally, in Chapter Three I draw on the cultural/normative discourses, practice and institutions that reflect gender partiality and their consistent inequality within the society, by explaining the main dynamics that produce unequal distributions of power, introducing the problematic both on a general, then on a more specific Third World and finally Caribbean reality. Gender differences are ideologically constructed in a way that the sexual and biological diversity is aligned with certain inequalities, which, in their turn, bring to the ideological transformation of biological female into the social feminine.

Gender is a linguistic artefact, a theoretical concept, a feminist invention, a quasi-object, shaped in order to deal with bodies, sexualities, the desire, power, and the politics of knowledge, although the popular, as well as intellectual, interpretation of gender was more or less synonymous with »woman«. In order to question women's subordination, indeed, it should be challenged on different discourses of sexuality and socio/cultural constructions of femininity. In the mythic imagination, more often than not, woman is an afterthought, created as a secondary category following the prior emergence of man.

The »par excellence« dimension of the construction of public and symbolic feminine is women's participation or absence in religious and ritual practices. Female metaphors and symbols are mainly reduced to their sexual function and consequentially, they have always had one-dimensional characters in mythology and ritual action, generating a further contradiction that is the construction of a dualist image of women (angel/witch) in the collective memory. That is to say that the conveyance of concepts and values expressed through oral, visual and ritual means, through the responses to or the manipulations of those messages, becomes a system of symbol, which is extremely gendered, for it is where the perpetuations or recreations of gender concept, symbolic meanings, social/structural divisions and individual gendered identity take place.

Gender discourses become central to the constitution of subjectivities through the production of powerful symbols, meanings and significance which have widespread ramifications, thereby deployed both by powerful collective actors and entities and by those in resistance or opposition to them, in order to instigate or to address social change. The act of bringing to light, better known as the act of »voicing« (Judith Butler, Gayatry Spivak...), challenges dichotomous representations, and, by so doing, it stresses the fact that women's realities are not locked within social, ethnic, classist and ideological representations, but, on the contrary they are fluid and sensible to a constant change.

The importance of cultural representation is referred to the process by which meanings are produced, and the ways in which images and texts reconstruct an ideological reality, rather than reflect the original sources that they represent. Consequently, in the case of women's struggles, the act of voicing through culture and cultural representations the ambivalence of their realities becomes a distinctly political and agentive process. Cultural productions, indeed, become the medium through which intimacy, the unvoiced marginalization and violence, the »natural« exclusion of women from the public becomes a political act, whose aim is to »feminize« and »equalize« the public male domain.

Since the men's attitudes toward women are symbolically projected in mythical narratives or in ritual performances, in Chapter Four, I elucidate on ways in which ritual practices are experienced and/or understood according to the cultural canon of the members of a given society, answering a need, an inner pulsing, an aspiration, a necessity for a defensive mechanism, or a yearning, on both personal and collective level. The play, in fact, has a subtle role in the formulation of a certain ethos – aggressive, devouring, anguishing, loving, or otherwise.

Ritual may lend continuity to life, the *status quo*, and may bring order to disorder, making comprehensible what goes beyond individual understanding and control. The popularity of certain rituals or myths at particular junctures in civilization explains the needs and deficiencies as well as the positive attributes of a given society, since the subtleties of society and culture may be better acknowledged and explained via the ambiguities, discrepancies, contradictions, and paradoxes expressed and exaggerated through ritual.

According to Lévi Strauss (1963), like in verbalized language myth and ritual are also a form of communication, in the sense that both project models of conceptual and intangible realities or human experiences, in a concrete and visible structure, which, in its turn, brings about reciprocal personal contact and preserves it. As Saussurre pointed out (1974), for the realization of a language, it is necessary to have a community of speakers, therefore language has a value only within a specific reality and never exists apart from the social fact. Indeed, if, generally speaking, a system is a matter of convention in a specific society and at specific time, then the mutability of the language is affected as well by historical (time) and social forces in an apparently contradictory way.

According to scholars like Van Genepp, Max Gluckman and Victor Turner, in order to try to dominate the imperative of biological changes, ritual practices become a necessity which accompany crisis. This passage of one status to another affects the social/individual removal from one status to other, by dramatizing the change, creating a liminal status, where the prior conditions are suspended for a circumscribed period of time, incorporating the individuals/group in the new social/natural dimension. The relationship between the ordinary and the non-ordinary in terms of social action is the result of a processing set of actions, performed mainly for their symbolic value mostly prescribed by a religion or by a tradition of a community, which becomes a fundamental part of human culture and a peculiar aid in the process of creating a sense of group identity and social bonds.

Although Turner, in the wake of Van Gennep's analysis, describes ritual as the element which mediates the transition of a community from the structure to the anti/structure, to a successive new structure, he also sees ritual as the subjunctive mood of a community- the ideal or symbolic layer of both: a real social process and liminality- as a restricted period of social limbo and an anti-structural moment of reversal which is the creative fond not only for ritual, but for culture in general.

In his analysis of ritual function within society, he extends the concept of *liminality* to include post-industrial, non ritual phenomena, by coining the term *liminoid* to apply to functional equivalent, making a distinction between the *liminal* phenomena, which are characteristic of the pre-industril society, and *liminoid*, which is the playlike feature of the post-industrial society. Religious obligation characterizes the liminal ('liturgy is derived from the Greek *'leos'* or *'laos'*, *'the people'*, and *'ergon'* 'work'), while »optation« characterizes the liminoid. Thus, in modern societies, cultural practices like Carnival are the dialectic between »is« and »may be«, the subjuntive mood of a given *communitas*, which through acting out the ideal of the community, is capable of being reflective and reflexive at the same time, creating the experience of the community, by arousing consciousness of ourselves as we see ourselves.

As I explained in Chapter Five, Carnival is a complex cultural and social phenomenon, based on the interrelationship of various codes (musical, verbal visual, gestural), whose actions form a pattern of symbols that dramatize shared values and beliefs, where the conjunction of ritual and play represent and exaggerate the lived social drama of individuals and communities. Thus, what Turner called social drama provides, in the form of religious plays, passion plays or carnival festivities, an insight of a different kind into the complexity of the dialectic relationship between ritual and social structure; that is, that the upside-down world of Carnival often may act as a form of protest against the existing social structure and contributes to social change.

Yet as the work of Bakhtin reminds us (1984), there was always an inherent possibility of unofficial subversion of authority and hierarchy through the alternative potential of the »culture of laughter«. Carnival, indeed, exemplified the complex and subtle dialectic between the official and the unofficial, becoming, according to David Gilmore, »this dialectic of culture and counter culture that endlessly renegotiates tradition«.[4]

According to Bakhtin, Carnival is an important primary form of human culture, because of its power to shape a complete world with its own space and time by reflecting and deconstructing wider social and political concerns such as class and gender divisions. The closed systems of social status and prestige that are put on public display in these particular carnival traditions do not simply illustrate the tensions between elitism and populism but also literally perform them; for these reasons, some scholars argue that rituals like carnival can help to change the *status quo*, while others suggest that they actually work to reinforce it.

All cultural practices (like theatre or secular festival) informed by ritual aim to do more than merely keep the spectator aesthetically engaged; ritual, in fact, is a central way of transforming and simultaneously maintaining the spiritual and common health of a society. The inversion and license of festival should be approached in terms of the general interrelationship between order and disorder, in the moral and social universe of the communities in which rites of reversal are conducted, for it is not simply a celebratory event that is bound in time and space, but also the source of a popular culture which

---

4 Gilmore, David (1998): »Carnival and Culture: Sex, Symbol, and Status in Spain«, Yale University Press, New Haven, Conn, London, p. 210

infiltrates official culture, permeating it with humour, irony and indeterminacy.

The nature of carnival is ambivalent; in fact, on one hand, folk culture appears periodically as a culture of laughter by means of an ensemble of rites and symbols, of a temporarily existing life form that enables carnival to take place; on the other hand, the principle of laughter which organizes carnival, is universal and transtemporal. Carnival, indeed, is social and antisocial, conservative and progressive, universal and specific, as Bakhtin asserted.

Thus, carnival rhetoric within its madcap ritual context has much to tell us about how the people experience and perceive their society and its traditions as elements of the felt life, becoming a »hyperbolic display of social relations«[5]. Carnival, in fact, beside its formal aspect of an occasion for maximum social chaos and licentious play, may be considered particularly ritualistic, because it draws together many social groups that are normally kept separate and create specific times and places where social differences are either laid aside or reversed for a more embracing experience of community.

Ritual based traditional enactments do not remain static, but transform to fit the contingencies of the new context; and, as I point out in Chapter Six, in the Caribbean one of the most obvious and prominent of these transformations of cultural signifiers is Carnival. In Trinidad Carnival is the fruit of local, global histories and the changing within these settings, - Spanish, British and French colonialism: the plantation system, slavery, indentured servitude, the international markets for sugar, cocoa, and oil; and anti-colonial agitation, decolonization, and the vicissitudes of state and nation formation after independence. Therefore the event has become both the reflection and the main expression of the entire society, nation and culture.

Carnival is considered the site around which different social identities are defined and confirmed. In Trinidad to *play mas* (to masquerade) signifies something besides the basic visual and performative fact of a person in a costume dancing and misbe-

---

5 Schechner, Richard (1993): »The Future of Ritual, Writings on Culture and Performance«, Routledge, New York and London, p. 51

having on the street, becoming, on the contrary, the mythopoesis of the new nation. Although carnival was introduced to Trinidad at the end of the eighteenth century by the French planters' elite and has incorporated elements from the European culture, it has managed throughout the history of Caribbean people and their achievement of independence, to reinterpret traditions belonging to an African past (see Chap. 6).

The present day carnival is the result of an ongoing process of hybridizations, adaptations, evolutions and cultural persistence, which mirrors, from different angles, a society whose search for a social integration continues to struggle with its pluralist tendencies dictated by a history of fragmentations, abuses of power, and its inevitable consequences.

Carnival becomes more than a display of parading floats and maskers; it is, in fact, the imaginative medium, the body of codes and conventions, of signs and signals, by which Trinidadians affirm their individuality within the society. Therefore, the unruly woman of the last two decades of Carnival might not just be pictured as an expression of sexuality with no object but itself and as the enactment of an absolute freedom rather than an inversion of cultural values, but as rehearsal performative act, that may be understood within a dramaturgy of power first exhibiting what it consigns to oblivion.

Caribbean women have lived in the periphery of history and society for a long time; until very recently they were defined by their relationship to men, in spite of their daily life, of their various ways of resistance, understanding and changing the world, which have been always devalued and considered insignificant. They have been invisible, unvoiced in the conventional history records, they have experienced –and the great majority is still experiencing- the »alienation within alienation«[6], as used by Kenneth Ramchand to picture the choked struggles of Caribbean women.

---

6 Kenneth, Ramchand (1983): »The West Indian Novel and its Background«, 2nd ed., Heinemann, London, p. 231, quoted by De Abruna, Niesen, Laura: »Twenty century Women Writer from the English Speaking Caribbean«, in Selwyn, R. Cudjoe (edited by) (1990): »Caribbean Women Writers«, Callaloux Publications, Wellesley, Massachussets, p. 86

In the West Indian society, where a number of cultural and socio-historical influences, dating back to the experience of slavery and Emancipation are held in a contradictory and transgressive tandem, gender relations and women status reflect the enormous complication which arose from the basic mismatch between the women's reality and the official dogmas systematically entrenched through formal education.

Caribbean society has commonly been characterized by a cultural dualism abstractly conceived as a structure of opposition that Peter Wilson (1973) calls »reputation« (which is referred to masculinity, spontaneity and »indigenous« practices and societal structure etc) and »respectability« (which accords to femininity, and normative and former colonial practices and institutions). On one hand, the ambivalence between women's life experiences and the ideologies in which they are trapped is translated in the carnevalesque women's subversion and appropriation of male-identified forms of sexual display that may actually serve to reinforce the patriarchal structures that it otherwise criticises. On the other hand, Carnival's emphasis on the mode of excess and reversal has always undermined the categories of social privilege, displaying a certain uniformity of identity within the process of masquerading and embodying an ongoing struggle against inequity and oppression, for in Trinidad entertainment has incorporated aspects of the sacred and ceremonial dances, by making them into voices of social protest and cultural renewal in the performative act of objectifying some other possibilities.

This transposition not only moves us beyond the rather unproductive debate over whether carnivals are politically progressive or conservative, it reveals that the underling structural features of carnival operate far beyond the strict confines of popular festivity and are intrinsic to the dialectics of social classification. The carnivalesque mediates between a classical/classificatory body and its mediation, its Others, what it excludes to create its identity as such. Not only is carnival, as part of the ideological production, generated out of conflict and contradictions, but it also addresses women, and to some extent men, on the issue of the contradictions that govern women's lives, redressing the limitations of the social structure, inevitably undertaking a politically integrative role, which may be part of the process of social change.

The validity of Carnival, as a higher performative genre, comic in desire and tragic in its outcome, depends on its capacity of absorbing and expressing the present, challenging the future by containing the past. Thus, the contemporary carnival is neither a sign of decline nor a rupture with the old, but the dynamic »magical mirror« (Turner 1986) of Trinidadians, which is rooted in the social reality and not imposed upon it.

I. DEFINITION OF POST-COLONIALISM: HYBRIDITY, MIMICRY AND NATIONAL IDENTITY

»Prospero, you are the master of illusion.
Lying is your trademark.
And you have lied so much to me
(lied about the world, lied about me)
that you have ended by imposing on me
an image of myself.
underdeveloped, you brand me, inferior,
That is the way you have forced me to see myself
I detest that image! What's more, it's a lie!
But now I know you, you old cancer,
and I know myself as well.«
(Aimé Césaire, A Tempest)

Post-Colonialism is an historical, political and socio-cultural phenomenon that comes after Colonialism. Although this may be an obvious implication of the term Post-Colonialism, such a common connotation has much to commend it, but that sense of an ending, of the completion of one period of history and the emergence of another, is hard to maintain in any simple or unproblematic fashion. Perhaps it is because of this consistency, still so manifest and problematic, that we do not discuss Post-Colonialism without dwelling first on what Colonialism really represented beyond the merely geographic features; in fact, Colonialism, Imperialism, and Post-Colonialism are indissolubly correlated.

According to Edward Said, the term Imperialism means »the practice, the theory and the attitudes of a dominating metropolitan centre ruling a distant territory«, while Colonialism, »which is almost always a consequence of Imperialism, is the implanting of settlements on distant territory«[7]. Modern Euro-

---

7   Said, Edward (1994): »Culture and Imperialism«, Vintage, London, p. 8

pean colonialism was distinctive and by far the most extensive of the different kinds of colonial contacts that have been a recurrent feature of human history: during the nineteenth century an unprecedented power was concentrated in Britain and in France and later, in other Western countries.

This century culminated with the rise of the West, and the western hegemony allowed the imperial metropolitan centres to acquire and accumulate territories on an amazing scale.

Colonialism was not an identical process in different parts of the world, but everywhere it implicated the original inhabitants and the newcomers into one of the most complex and traumatic relationships humanity ever experienced. Neither colonialism nor imperialism are pure acts of expansion and acquisition of new lands, but, in a quite systematic way, they affected other peculiar aspects belonging, for instance, to the socio-cultural sphere of both counter-parties, as for the settler colonies, and the »centre« of the empire, that is, the »running protagonist« to the conquest of the »New World«.

Right through modern Imperial time and places, the Western *modus operandi* has radically changed and restructured the domain that we now call Society. The Martinique poet and politician Aimé Césaire describes the colonizing process as:

»et je dis que la colonization à la civilization, la distance est infinie; que de toutes les expéditions coloniales accumulées, de tous les statuts coloniaux élaborés, de toutes les circulaires ministérielles expédiées, on ne saurait réussir une seule valeur humaine.*«[8]

According to Césaire, the Martiniquen psychiatric Franz Fanon, in his famous book »Black Skin, White Masks«, by taking his analysis to the reign of both the colonized populations' and the masters' psyche, had several times stressed this dehumanized aspect of colonialism, arguing that colonialism created an infe-

---

8 Césaire, Aimé (1955): »Discourse sur le Colonialism«, Presence Africaine, Paris, p. 8

* My translation: »And I say that between colonization and civilization, the distance is infinite; that of all the accumulated colonial expeditions, of all the elaborated colonial regulations, the dispatched ministerial letters, no one was able to attain a single human value.«

riority complex through the oppression of the local and cultural distinctiveness.

Ideology does not concern just the political sphere, but it is related to all our mental structures, our beliefs, the concepts and the ways of expressing our relationships with the outside world. The stratification of a society in classes, the subsistence of a superior race (of course white and belonging to the western world) and of an inferior (black/not European) the binary opposition of the humanity in »Us« as the representative of civilization and »Other« as primitive and uncivilized, are actually the result of complicated and lengthy cultural elaborations, shaped by the necessity of giving convincing motivations that legitimated the abuse of power and the political and cultural and economic dominion of one population over another. Science, literature and the other forms of art had the task to sponsor the empire policy by divulging its ideology, and, at the same time, providing valid excuses.

English nationalism, for example, was established on differentiations which divided not only the Europeans and the Blacks (the natives) but also the English people, from the Italians and the Irish; in other words, these cultural distinctions were essential to the process of rationalizing the aggressive nationalism which alimented the British expansion overseas. In fact, even if the main battle was over the land, all the issues -concerning who owned those territories, who had the right to settle, who made them profitable, and who, at the end, won them back- were reflected, contested and, even for a time, decided through culture.

Language and literature were both engaged in the construction of the binary opposition of the »European« and the others »non European« that, according to what Said asserts in »Orientalism«, is part of the creation of the colonial authority. Literary texts were fundamental in the process of forming colonial discourses, principally because of their eligibility in influencing either the imagination and the individuals (since Plato, it has been known that literature mediates between reality and imagination) and of showing the complex articulation between the single individual, the social contest, and the language. In other words, the formation of an Empire, in order to be achieved, has to be supported by the idea of having an empire-as Joseph Conrad seemed to have profoundly understood- and then, in order to obtain it, the whole groundwork has to be made through culture.

Imperialism, considered as a practice with a fundamental cultural dimension, represents such a general and, at the same time, circumstantial phenomenon, that is not possible to discuss places laid one upon another, intertwined stories and experiences- shared by men and women, whites and non whites, from the centre to the periphery, in the past as in the present and in the future- without dwelling on it from the unitary perspective of the secular human history. Indeed, if we agree that the history of Europe for the past few centuries has been profoundly shaped by the colonial interests, then there is a logic, in which much of the cultural expressions produced during that time can be said to be colonial, or, vice versa and as a consequence, post-colonial, even if only tangentially so.

Culture offers one of the most important ways in which these »new« perceptions are expressed, and it is through the various languages of culture such as literature, painting, sculpture, music and dance, that the day to day realities experienced by the colonised have been most powerfully encoded and so profoundly influential. So, we use the term Postcolonial to cover all culture affected by the imperial process from the moment of colonization up to the present day, for there is a continuity of preoccupations throughout the historical process initiated by European aggression. Postcolonial studies developed as a way of addressing the cultural production of those societies affected by the historical phenomenon of colonialism.

Despite the reservations and debates, the research in Postcolonial Studies is growing for postcolonial critics allow for a wide-ranging investigation into power relations in various contexts. The formation of an empire, the impact of colonization on history, economy, science, and culture, the cultural productions of postcolonial societies, feminism and post-colonialism, agency for marginalized people, and the state of post-colonies in contemporary economy and cultural contexts are some broad topics in the field.

The imposition of a unique meaning to the decolonization process would efface all the differences and gradations encoded in the word Post-Colonialism. Thus, it is not enough to set out a limit to postcolonial studies by focusing the analysis strictly on historical explanations and motivations, as it would not be possible to satisfy completely the various issues concerning society, culture, the economical and political aspects of this complex phenomenon.

On one hand, Post-Colonialism investigates the kind of violence which was often part of the cultural interaction, seeking for solutions that should be interlaced with representations which the new populations, victims of past abuses can be identified with. On the other hand, it suggests models as a way of directing the efforts toward a common resolution of the eternal conflicts between different ethnic groups, considering the nature of identity in contests where these groups may find a common point of contact and interact with each other.

In this regard it was never conceived of as a grand theory, but as a methodology: in order analyse the many strategies by which the colonised have engaged imperial discourse and second in order to study the ways in which many of those strategies are shared by colonised societies, which re-emerge in very different political and cultural circumstances. Thus, the principal aim of postcolonial studies is the attempt to understand how postcolonial culture resisted the power of colonial domination in ways so subtle that they transformed both coloniser and colonised, for culture describes the myriad of ways in which a group of people make a sense of, represent and inhabited its world, and as such can never be destroyed. From an historical point of view, postcolonial studies concern the movements for the national freedom which brought the colonies to emancipation from the European dominium on a vast part of the globe.

In 1946, after the end of the Second World War, an era of worldwide decolonization began. The two-fifths of the inhabited earth that made up the British empire, together with former colonial possessions of other European powers, became independent of their metropoles. The year 1947 was the beginning of this process with the acquisition of independency from Southern Asia, which until that moment has always been considered the »Jewel in the Crown«[9] of the British Empire. Subse-

---

9   Schwarz, Henry: »Mission Impossible: Introducing the Postcolonial Studies in Us Academy«, in Schwarz, Henry/ Ray, Sangeeta

quently, in a period of forty years, one nation after the other gained the freedom that was unfairly denied them for centuries, gradually dismantling the structure of the direct colonial control. These »new nations« were joined by most of Africa and the rest of the colonized world in the late 1950s and 1960s. Jointly these regions became known as the Third World as distinct from the First World (the West) and the Second World (the USSR). Presently, circa 75% of the people living in the world have had their lives moulded by the experience of colonialism. It is more evident how important this has been in the political and economic spheres, but its general influence on the perceptual frameworks of contemporary people is often less clear.

Much discussion surrounds which countries ought to be considered part of the postcolonial world. Since former states of the Soviet Union have adopted the expression to refer to post-glasnost, post-colonialism is not more specific to a particular imperial regime, even though it often refers to the former colonies of the British Empire. The British Empire was the largest modern empire, and its vestiges still exist today in a reconfigured organisation of former commonwealth states, which oversees political alliances and trade treaties among the ex-colonies.

Today a great number of scholars suggest that it would be more constructive to think about post-colonialism not just as something that comes after colonialism, or that signifies its cessation, but, in a flexible way, as the contestation of the colonial dominium and legacy. This perspective allowed the inclusion within postcolonial phenomenon of populations which are geographically dispersed because of their colonial past. Indeed we should ask ourselves not only when post-colonialism began, but as well where we may locate it.

By writing the conclusion of her book »The Caribbean Postcolonial: social equality, post-nationalism and cultural hybridity«, Shalini Puri, in order to explain what is post-colonialism, and above all, from which perspective (first world/ third world context) it should be interrogated, invokes a particular event in which Gayatri Spivak, one of the most prominent names in the postcolonial critic, participated. The location was the Centre for

---

(edited by) (2000): »A Companion to Postcolonial Studies«, Blackwell Publishers Ltd, Oxford, p. 1

Historical studies at the elite Jawahralal Nehru University of New Delhi, where Spivak, Professor at Columbia University and holding a visiting professorship at the Nehur University, was interviewed by three Indian women, all currently professors of English literature in various universities in Delhi:

»The interview is interesting and significant for the range of topics covered: the nature of postcolonial intellectual, the use of First World theory, the women's movement, and the implications of teaching English literature in post colonial countries. Instead of being a commemoration of Spivak's triumphant homecoming however, the interview is fraught with tension and undercurrents of discord between her and the three Indian professors. As the interview begins, Spivak is asked to comment on the difference between the way she, 'a post colonial diasporic Indian who seeks to decolonize the mind' perceives herself, and the way she has constituted them, that is a native intellectuals'. Spivak's response is coded with a certain degree of dismay at the lines so sharply drawn by the Delhi –based professors. Their question reveals that she is not one of them, a charge that could be seen as calling into question the identity Spivak relies upon as a practising academician, cultural and postcolonial theorist in the US. She responds, 'your description of how I constituted you, equally with the diasporic Indian, as a post-colonial intellectual'.«[10]

Many of the analysis concerning postcolonial societies essentially assume colonialism as the unique history of these societies. But, what about before colonialism? That is, which ideologies, which native practices existed beside it, and influenced it? Colonialism, in fact, did not develop on a *tabula rasa*, so it could not be considered as an explanation for everything concerning postcolonial societies. The food, music, the languages, the arts of any culture which we call postcolonial, evoke a specific past, or show shades that may not be traced back to colonialism.

Many of these settled colonies now possess a linguistic heritage that is based on the English language, most of them continue to engage with the imperial experience, although they have achieved their political independence. Through culture,

---

[10] Puri, Shalini (2004): » The Caribbean Postcolonial: social equality, post-nationalism, and cultural hybridity«, Palgrave Macmillan, New York, Basingstoke, pp. 177-78

education, and more specific, the language and the literary canon, the body of the British texts, which too frequently still acts as a touchstone of taste and value, the weight of the past and antiquity continue to dominate cultural production in a large part of the postcolonial world.

The Caribbean writer George Lamming in the »Occasion for Speaking«, by recalling the publication of his first book »In the Castle of My Skin«, gives a clear example on how the myth of Britain is still deeply rooted in the common imagination of the former colonies:

»I remembered how pleased I was to learn that my first book, in the Castle of my Skin, had been bought by an American publisher. [...] It was the money I was thinking of to the exclusion of the book's critical reputation in America. The book had had an important critical press in England; its reputation here was substantial; so I could make no difference what America thought [...]. This is what I mean by the myth. It has little to do with lack of intelligence. It has nothing to do with one's origins in class.
It is deeper and more natural. It is akin to the nutritive function of milk which all sorts of men received at birth. It is myth as the source of spiritual foods absorbed, and learnt for exercise in the future.
This myth begins in the West Indian from the earliest stages of his education.«[11]

Thus, Post-Colonialism inevitably addresses reactions to colonialism in a contest that is not necessarily determined by temporal constraints; postcolonial cultural phenomena then become expressions of resistance to imperialism.

Culture has the political capacity of dismantling the hegemonic boundaries and the determinants that create unequal relations of power based on binary oppositions such as »us and them«, »first world and third world«, »white and black«, »coloniser and colonised«. The central strategy in transforming the imperialistic culture is the seizing of the self representation; the underlying of all economic, political and social resistances is the

---

[11] Lamming, George (1960): »Occasion for speaking«, in Aschcroft, Bill/Garreth Griffiths/Tiffin Helen (edited by) (2004): » The Postcolonial Studies Reader«, Routledge, New York and London, p. 13

struggle over representation (that is the process of giving a concrete form to ideological concepts) that occurs in language, writing and other forms of cultural production.

Cultural representations were central first to the process of colonizing other lands, and then again to the process of obtaining independence from the master principally by deconstructing and subverting the canonical assumptions of culture imposed by the colonizers. Post-Colonialism, in fact, has often been concerned with the ways and extents to which culture and its representations are crucial to an identity formation and the construction of subjectivity.

To assume control over a territory or a nation was not only to exert political or economic power, it was also to have imaginative command; the forming of an identity is, most of the times, strictly connected with the idea of belonging to a common nation, an »imagined community« (Anderson 1983) which has to be endowed with an historical, racial and cultural unity. We are all still the heirs of a way of thinking by which everyone is defined by the nation which belongs to and, in its turn, the nation bases its own authority on a presumed, but also uninterrupted, tradition.

Post-Colonialism, indeed, may not be seen as a passive acceptance of the new global system, nevertheless it constitutes a critical answer to those conditions. Nowadays, the so called postcolonial states, in order to obtain a complete autonomy, have to dwell with an adversary characterized by an extended power (of course in terms of institutions and practices), which is one of the main tasks of globalization's principals.

Those countries which struggled for independence shaped the »new« states on the Western/European »Idea« of Nation. In the XIX century Europe was the cradle of national consciousness and nationalism. After the Napoleonic wars, inspired by the idea of a world empire, there began the wars of national liberation, whilst national self-awareness grew. National states crystalised into shape. The sense of history, the memory of the past, the romantic theories of returning to the origins, were functional to the political discourse concerning the idea of a nation building.

In the ode »Marzo 1821«, the poet Alessandro Manzoni manifested on behalf of the entire Italian population, who was seeking for freedom and unity, the national sentiment, which might demonstrate how the idea of nation was so profoundly forged during the romantic era:

»una d'arme, di lingua, di altare,
di memorie, di sangue, di cor«
(Alessandro Manzoni: Marzo 1821)[12]

Akin to imperialism, but on a different scale, the western nationalism of the XIX century was formed via literature, was fed by romanticism and, as a consequence, was abstract. Anticolonial struggles, therefore, had to create new and powerful identities for colonised people, challenging colonialism at political, cultural and emotional levels.

The ideology of a nation formation is based on the unifying signifiers of culture (religion, language, tradition…) history and race, which have to be re- discovered in a remote past, mythical and ancestral. The history of modern cultural phenomena is strictly interconnected with the development of a »cultural nationalism«, which, in its turn, pursued two main objectives: first the search and definition of a national canon, second the defence and preservation of its value, authority and aesthetic autonomy. Nationalism generates nations and not vice versa.

No doubt nationalism utilizes the pre-existent cultural proliferations, that is a historical heritage and, although it is actuated in a selective way, most of the time this process radically transforms them. From this prospective we can say, indeed, that nationalism is substantially the general imposition of a superior culture upon a society in which previously inferior cultures ruled the life of the majority and, in some cases, of the whole population.

The fusion of *voluntas* (will), culture and State becomes then the norm, which could parallely turn into a process of a cultural/ social auto-adoration, sometimes violent and virulent too, anyhow always openly recognized. In this regard, Eric Hobsbawm, by describing the nation formation in the European

---

12 My translation: »One of weapons, language, altar, /of memories, blood, heart.«

contest of the XVIII-XIX century and assuming the Nation as an »Invented Tradition«, wrote:

»We should not be misled by a curious, but understandable, paradox; modern nations and all their impedimenta generally claim to be opposite of novel, namely rooted in the remotest antiquity, and the opposite of constructed, namely human communities so 'natural' as require no definition other than self assertion. [...]
And just because so much of what subjectively makes up the modern 'nation' consists of such constructs and is associated with appropriate and, in general, fairly recent symbols or suitably tailored discourse (such as 'national history'), the national phenomenon cannot be adequately investigated without careful attention to the 'invention of tradition.«[13]

In the Wretched of the Earth Franz Fanon explains with a veiled irony, which is often a sign of a bitter reality, the simple reason for this frantic search for ancestral origins that is the basis of the re-building of a new National Culture.

»The passion with which native intellectuals defend the existence of their national culture may be a source of amazement; but those who condemn this exaggerated passion are strangely apt to forget that their own psyche and their own selves are conveniently sheltered behind a French or German culture which has given full proof of its existence and which is uncontested.
I am ready to concede that on the plane of factual being the past existence of an Aztec civilization does not change anything very much in the diet of the Mexican peasant of today. I admit that all the proofs of a wonderful Songhais civilization will not change the fact that today Songhais are under-fed and illiterate, thrown between sky and water with empty heads and empty eyes. But it has been remarked several times that this passionate search for a national culture which existed before the colonial era finds its legitimate reason in the anxiety shared by native intellectuals to shrink away from that western culture in which they all risk being swamped. Because they realize they are in danger of

---

13 Hobsbawm, Eric: »Introduction: Inventing Traditions«, in Hobsbawm, Eric/Ranger, Terence (1983): »The invention of Tradition«, Cambridge University Press, Cambridge, pp. 13-14

losing their lives and thus becoming lost to their people, these men, hotheaded and with anger in their hearts, relentlessly determine to renew contact once more with the oldest and most pre-colonial springs of life of their people.«[14]

The nation is imagined and mythicized, it is narrated via allusive and symbolic figures. The idea of »Nation«, a concept of a shared community and traditions (that is, according to Malinowsky »a form of collective adaptation of a community to its surroundings«[15]) has enabled the postcolonial societies to invent a self image through which they could act to liberate themselves from the imperial oppression. According to Fanon's assumption:

»All of that, exhumed from the past, spread with its insides out, made it possible for me to find a valid historic place. The white man was wrong, I was not a primitive, not even a half-man, I belonged to a race that had already been working in gold and silver two thousand years ago.«[16]

Modern art, philosophy, theatre, literature, could not be interpreted as simple adjustments or continuations of Europeans models. Post-colonial culture is the result of complex evolutions in which different cultures developed in totally diverse contexts through mutual interaction, interlacing and encounters. According to Bill Ashcroft, we may consider postcolonial phenomena as »cross cultural« because »they negotiate a gap between 'worlds', a gap in which the simultaneous process of abrogation and appropriation continually strive to define and determinate their practice«[17].

---

14 Fanon, Franz (1967): »The Wretched of the Earth«, Penguin Books, Harmondsworth, Middlesex England, , p. 168
15 Talal, Asad: » From the History of Colonial Anthropology to the Anthropology of the Western Hegemony«, in Vincent, Joan (2002): »The Anthropology of Politics«, Blackwell Publishing Ltd, Oxford, p. 135
16 Fanon, Franz (1986): »Black Skin, Withe Masks«, Pluto Press, London, p. 131
17 Aschcroft, Bill/Garreth, Griffiths/Tiffin, Helen (1994): »The Empire Writes Back, Theory and Practice in Post-colonial Literature«, Routledge, London and New York, p. 39

Homi Bhabha calls this gap »Third Space«, that is, a space in-between which »carries the burden of the meaning of culture«[18]. ccording to Homi Bhabha, all cultural statements and systems are constructed in this contradictory and ambivalent space, in which cultural identity always emerges.

He calls this process of reconstruction Mimicry, assuming that:

»the colonial mimicry is the desire for a reformed, recognizable Other, as a subject of a difference that is almost the same, but not quite. Which is to say that the discourse of mimicry is constructed around an ambivalence; in order to be effective, mimicry must continually produce its slippage, its excess, its difference.«[19]

From a cultural perspective decolonization determined firstly a dismantlement of the European canons, and then, secondly, their re-appropriation and their re-use in a »new« contest; moreover the whole process was supported by the claiming and rediscovery of an ancestral/ pre-colonial past. Inevitably, post-colonial culture is considered hybrid, characterized by a dialectic relation between a dominant European and the natives' culture, which has been for too long time suppressed by the weight of a suffered past in search for a new own totally independent identity.

The idea of hybridity underlies the attempts of stressing the variety of cultures in the colonial and postcolonial process in expressions of syncrety, cultural synergy and trans-culturation. Hybridity occurs in postcolonial societies both as a result of conscious moments of cultural suppression, for example, when the colonial power invades to consolidate political and economic control, or when settler invaders dispossess indigenous people and force them to assimilate new social patterns, as in the last decades of the XX century and, of course, nowadays, when patterns of immigration from the metropolitan societies and from other imperial areas of influence continue to produce complex trans-cultural interlaces.

---

18 Bahbha., Homi K. (1988): »Cultural diversity and Cultural Differences«, in Aschcroft/ Garreth/Tiffin (2004): op. cit., p. 209
19 Bhabha (1994): op.cit., p. 86

The characteristic of its hybridised nature is the mutuality of the process, that is to say the transaction of the postcolonial world is not a one way process, in which oppression obliterates the oppressed, or the colonizer silences the colonized in absolute terms. The great peculiarity of postcolonial phenomena consists in its capacity of transforming and »personalizing« expressions of different cultures into a definition of an Own Culture, that is, into a new »own« representation of the »Self« and the »Other«. It emphasises how hybridity and the power it releases may allow a means of the replication of the binary categories of the past and develop new anti-monolithic models of cultural exchange and growth.

If we assume that all cultural statements and systems are formulated within this contradictory and ambivalent space of enunciation, we will understand the reason why hierarchical claiming of an intrinsic cultural originality and purity are nonsense. The cultural variety and mutuality are recognition of cultural contents and habits »already performed«, which, if we consider them within the temporal frame of relativism, produce liberal notions of multiculturalism and cultural interactions of human culture. Indeed, we should now understand and agree with Bhabha's conclusions on what he calls »Third Space«:

»For a willingness to descend in that territory- where I have led you- may reveal that the theoretical recognition of the split-space of enunciation may open the way to conceptualizing an *inter*national culture, based not on the *exoticism** of multiculturalism or the diversity of cultures, but on the inscription and articulation of culture's *hybridity* , to that end we should remember that it is the 'inter'- the cutting edge- of translation and negotiation, the *in-between* space - that carries the burden of the meaning of culture. It makes it possible to begin envisaging national, anti-nationalist histories of the 'people'. And by exploring this Third Space, we may elude the politics of polarity and emerge as the others of our selves.«[20]

Furthermore, collective memory follows the logic of myth by translating abstract concepts into images people can identify

---

*   My emphasis.
20   Bhabha (1994): op.cit, pp. 38-39

with, which is, in other words, the modes of expression of a colonial past and a post-colonial reality. This process is performed through dreams, imagination and the magic:

»- D'ora in avanti sarò io a descrivere le città e tu verificherai se esistono e se sono come io le ho pensate. Comincerò a chiederti d'una città a scale, esposta a scirocco, su un golfo a mezzaluna. [...]
- Sire, eri distratto. Di questa città appunto ti stavo raccontando quando m'hai interrotto.
- La conosci? Dov'è? Qual è il suo nome?
- Non ha nome né luogo. Ti ripeto la ragione per cui la descrivo: dal numero delle città immaginabili occorre escludere quelle i cui elementi si sommano senza un filo che li connetta, senza una regola interna, una prospettiva, un discorso. E' delle città come dei sogni: tutto l'immaginabile può essere sognato, ma anche il sogno più inatteso è un rebus che nasconde un desiderio, oppure il suo rovescio, una paura. Le città come i sogni sono costruite di desideri e di paure, anche se il filo del loro discorso è segreto, le loro regole assurde, le prospettive ingannevoli, e ogni cosa ne nasconde un'altra [....].«[21]

---

21 Calvino, Italo (1972): »Le città invisibili«, Mondatori, Milano, pp. 43-44
»From now on I shall describe the cities and you will tell me if they exist and are as I have conceived them. I shall begin by asking you of a city with stairs, exposed to the sirocco, on a half-moon bay [...]«
»Sire, your mind has been wandering. This is precisely the city I was telling you about when you interrupted me.«
»You know it? Where is it? What is its name?«
»It has neither name nor place. I shall repeat the reason why I was describing it to you: from the number of imaginable cities we must exclude those whose elements are assembled without a connecting thread, an inner rule, a perspective, a discourse. With cities, it is as with dreams: everything imaginable can be dreamed, but even the most unexpected dream is a rebus that conceal a desire or, its reverse, a fear. Cities, like dreams, are made of desires and fears, even if the thread of their discourse is secret, their rules are absurd, their perspectives deceitful, and everything conceals something else.«, Calvino, Italo (1997): »Invisible Cities«, Vintage, London, pp 43-44

In this regard Salman Rushdie, if he were in Marco Polo's place, would say to the imperator Kublai Khan that the act of telling is a lie to say the truth[22]. Thus, the »social« construction of the unreality might be one of the principal scopes of postcolonial culture. According to Michael Dash:

> »If there is one sound idea that the ideology of 'negritude' puts forward, it is certainly the notion of the double alienation of the black man- that is a belief that the problem is more than political and economic, that there was a psychological and spiritual reconstruction that should also take place. However, it was difficult for them to provide a solution to the problem of spiritual loss to the extent that any notions of survival or emergence of a Third World personality were totally neglected. This is the essential difference between 'Marvellous Realism' and 'Negritude'- for the former stresses patterns of emergence from the continuum of history.«[23]

So, to sum up, within the evolution of postcolonial culture we may evaluate three dominant features which are strictly correlated and common to every postcolonial society. The first one is the insistence on the right of re-interpreting integrally and coherently the human/ colonial history of its own community, in order to recover and give back to the people their »imprisoned« nation.

One of the first duties of the culture of resistance was, for example, the act of re-appropriation, re-naming and re-inhabiting the land, which was then accompanied by an entire range of ulterior information, re-discoveries and identifications set upon sources poetically projected. The search of authenticity and national roots, which had to be more congenial than the one given by colonial history, of a new pantheon of heroes and in a few rare cases heroines, myths, religions and legends were possible through the re-appropriation of the land by its people. Partially this process gets stuck when the re-birth of the »new« culture, based on ancestral archetypes, inevitably meets and

---

22 Quoted by Albertazzi, Silvia (2000): »Lo sguardo dell'Altro«, Carrocci Editore, Roma, p.86.
23 Dash, Michael (1974): »Maravellous Realism, The Way Out of Negritude«, in Aschroft/ Griffiths/ Tiffin (2004): op.cit., p. 199

melts with the culture of the masters; one clarifying example is Naipaul's representation of India as a culture which has to refer to the Mother country for its own identity and maybe for its »Englishness«.

The second main point is the idea that resistance, far from being just a reaction to imperialism, represents an alternative (in the sense of mirrored) way of understanding the human history. For this reason it is of great importance to determine how deeply this »alternative conception« is constructed on the abolition of cultural boundaries.

The »Writing back«, like the title of a famous book[*], is an essential component of this practice; that is, to formulate an answer to the metropolitan cultures and, at the same time, to undermine the European narrations and cultural assumptions on the so called »Third World«, in order to substitute them with a stronger and playful »cultural imagination«.

The conscious effort of penetrating into the western cultural discourse, of mixing it up, of transforming it so deeply that it has to recognize the forgotten and suppressed stories of the »subalterns« (referring to the meaning used by Spivak), is called by Edward Said »The Voyage in«[24]. The third aspect is the act of taking distance from a separatist nationalism for a more integrative vision of the »human global community«. His explanation lays on the assumption that the history of each culture is a history of »trans-cultural loans«, that is to say that culture has not to be understood as an impermeable propriety, made by lending or borrowing loans with debtors and creditors, but as a complex and mutual whole of common experiences, encounters and various inter-dependences between different cultures.

---

[*] Ashcroft/Griffiths/Tiffin: »The Empire Writes Back: Theory and Practices in post-colonial culture«
24 Said (1994): op.cit., p. 261

II. Re-Inventing Culture: The Caribbean Example.
Introducing the Caribbean: History and Society

»I accept this archipelago of the Americas. I say to the ancestor who sold me, and to the ancestor who bought me, I have no father, I want no such father, although I can understand you, black ghost, white ghost, when you both whisper 'history', for if I attempt to forgive you both I am falling into your idea of history which justifies and explains and expiates, and it is not mine to forgive, my memory cannot summon any filial love, since your features are anonymous and erased and I have no wish and no power to pardon. You were when you acted your roles, your given, historical roles of slave seller and slave buyer, men acting as a man, and also you, father in the filth ridden gut of the slave ship, to you they were also men, acting as men with the cruelty of men, your fellowman and tribesman not move or hovering with hesitation about your common race any longer than my other bastard ancestor hovered with his whip, but to your inwardly forgiven grandfathers, I, like the most honest of my race, give a strange thanks. I give the strange and bitter and yet ennobling thanks for the monumental groaning and soldering of two great worlds, like the halves of a fruit seamed by its own bitter juice, that exiled from your own Edens you have placed me in the wonder of another, and that was my inheritance and your gift.«[25]
(Derek Walcott, The Muse of History)

The history of the Caribbean is rich with tumultuous and cruel battles of conquest, forced migrations and indentured labour, blended cultures, ethnic and natural diversity. The present aspect of the islands has been shaped largely by events which

---

25 In: Ashcroft/Griffiths/Tiffin (2004): op. cit., pp. 373-374

took place after the arrival of the first European discoveres in Columbus's fleet in 1492.

The Caribbean has been less of a meeting place than a corridor. The islands were occupied by colonists who were tied to Europe. The gravitational pull of Europe to the east was balanced by a corresponding pull to the west. The Caribbean waterways have linked Europe with Latin America, Spain with the Phillipines, New England with California, South America with the United States and Canada. They have divided the Caribbean countries shore from shore, island from island.

Knowing the history of the Caribbean region goes a long way towards understanding its people. Each island has a unique cultural identity shaped by the European, the African heritage of slaves, and the enduring legacies of East Indian or more generally Asiatic population.

The almost total destruction of the autochthonous was an early consequence of European colonization during the sixteenth and seventeenth centuries. The conquerors were Western Europeans: Spanish, English, Dutch, and French. Then came the Africans, captured, transported, sold and enslaved on New World estates during three hundred years. The peoples who inhabit the islands migrated or were deliberately transplanted from the Old World. They came from Europe, Africa and Asia, bringing with them their religious beliefs, their languages and their social habits. Today the evidence of this transplanting of social institutions can be seen on every hand in the Caribbean.

The general picture of the Caribbean islands -scattered for 2,500 miles of sea between Mexico's Yucatan Peninsula with Cuba as the first island and the north east coast of South America with Trinidad as the last of the Atoll- might be seen as a mosaic of various people with different cultures, backgrounds and heritage who shared their lives and experiences throughout the history of the Western overseas expansion and hegemony, set against a backdrop of crystal clear waters and perpetual sunshine, which ironically is fixed in the common imagination as a unique Paradise on Earth.

Caribbean space is difficult to define, its cultures precarious and diverse, and the views of ruling and aspiring elites dominate the interpretation of the past. This task has been further complicated by the problems of language. Linguistic barriers have encouraged nationalism, insularity and old imperialistic enclaves. Since the 1950s, efforts have been made to reverse this reality and to rewrite the history of the region, this time from the inside.

This has been a problematic undertaking; but, although Caribbean societies have not undergone the same historical process, because of the very diverse origins of the populations, the complicated history of the European cultural impositions and the absence of a firm continuity of culture of the colonial power, there exists an undeniably common identity, born of the climate and of their history, which undoubtedly unifies these lands and peoples. That is to say, according to Sidney W. Minzt, that:

»One of the ways to clarify the importance of the Caribbean islands is to limn their social and cultural characteristics against a backdrop of regional history, much of their commonality, their meaning as a bloc of societies, is the result of demonstrably parallel historical experiences during more than four centuries of powerful (though intermittent and whimsical) European influence.«[26]

By analysing the Antilles in term of a »multidimensional continuum«, rather than an undifferentiated grouping, Mintz traced the Caribbean regional commonality in nine major features:

(1) Lowland, subtropical, insular ecology;
(2) The swift extirpation of native populations;
(3) The early definition of the islands as a sphere of European overseas agricultural capitalism, based primarily on sugarcane, African slaves, and plantation system;
(4) The concomitant development of insular social structures in which internally differentiated local community organization was slight, and national class groupings usually took on a bipolar form, sustained by overseas domination, sharply differentiated access to land, wealth and political power, and the use of physical differences as status markers;

---

26 Mintz (1971): op.cit., p. 18

(5) The continuous interplay of plantations and small scale yeoman agriculture, with accompanying social-structural effects;
(6) The successive introduction of massive and »foreign« populations into the lower sectors of insular social structures, under conditions of extremely restricted opportunities for upward economic, social, or political mobility;
(7) The prevailing absence of any ideology of national identity that could serve as a goal for mass acculturation;
(8) The persistence of colonialism, and of the colonial ambience, longer than in any other outside western Europe;
(9) A high degree of individualization –particularly economic individualization- as an aspect of Caribbean social organization.[27]

Indeed, despite the background of small dimensions and poverty, the Caribbean region comprised some of the most lucrative colonies in the world history. Furthermore the economic success of colonialism in the Caribbean colonies was strictly related to the growth of European »motherlands« and the enormous expansion of the European industry in the eighteenth and nineteenth centuries. The economic exploitation was supported by a highly industrial organization, that is to say, that in the Caribbean region, the plantation system was a capitalistic form of development.

The plantation society, sometimes referred to as the slave society, was a society by default. It was never consciously engineered to represent a microcosm of Africa or Europe or Asia or even indigenous America. It was designed for the efficient production and organized export of plantation staples: tobacco, sugar, cotton, cacao, and coffee. The Antigua writer Jamaica Kinkaid, in her essay »A Small Place«, comments sarcastically on this reality, by pointing out that:

»do you know why people like me are shy about being capitalist? Well, it is because we, for as long as we have known you, were capital, like bales of cotton and sacks of sugar, and you were the commanding cruel capitalists, and the memory of this is so strong, the experience so recent,

---

27 Ibid, p. 20

that we can quite bring ourselves to embrace this idea that you think so much of.«[28]

Plantation societies were, indeed, inherently of man as much as agricultural resources. Imposed on the initial settler societies, this capitalistic approach deeply changed the basic economy, the demographic structure, the internal politics and social relationships, and consequently the relationship of the region with the wider world.

The eighteenth century brought about a turning point in the Caribbean history, when a massive number of enslaved Africans were brought to the islands in order to supply to the urgent claim of labour. European importers demanded high quantities of sugar, the product of sugar cane, which grew easily in the Caribbean temperate weather. As the demand of sugar increased, so did the demand for plantation labour.

The indigenous were the Europeans' original slaves but they were quickly dying out. By this time slavery was a fixture in European and Arab countries. To continue this grievous trend in the Caribbean, Friar Bartoleme de las Casas of Hispaniola suggested enslaving Africans. Hence, many new slaves were brought from Africa's Guinea coast.

»The slave trade scoured the coasts of Guinea. As they devastated an area they moved westward and then south, decade after decade, past the Niger down to the Congo coast, past Loango and Angola, round the Cape of Good Hope, and, by the 1789, even as far as Mozambique on the eastern side of Africa. Guinea remained their chief hunting ground.«[29]

They were taken from their homes by slave-raiding parties, which were often endorsed by the local government. They were shipped to the West Indies via the notorious Middle Passage- a horrendous mode of transport in which slaves were packed into

---

28 Kinkaid, Jamaica (1988): »A Small Place«, Penguin Books, London, pp. 36-37
29 James, C.L.R.(1989): »The Black Jacobins, Toussaint L'Ouvertur and the San Domingo Revolution«, Allison & Busby Book, London, p. 6

the ship's hold so tightly that they could not move freely and sometimes suffocated to death. On average, twelve percent of slaves died on the trip; those who survived were fed, »oiled«, and paraded through the streets to the slave market where they were auctioned off and traded for liquor, guns, and other goods.

»The slaves were collected in the interior, fastened one to the other in columns, loaded with heavy stones of 40 or 50 pounds in weight to prevent attempts at escape, and then marched the long journey to the sea, sometimes hundreds of miles, the weakly and sick dropping to die in the African jungle.
Some were brought to the coast by canoe. [...]
At the slave ports they were penned into 'trunks' for the inspections of the buyers.[...]
Outside in the harbour, waiting to empty the 'trunks' as they filled, was the captain of the slave-ship, with so clear a conscience that one of them, in the intervals of waiting to enrich British capitalism with the profit of another valuable cargo, enriched British religion by composing the hymn: 'How Sweet the Name of Jesus sounds'.
On the ship the slave were packed in the hold on galleries one above the other [...] they could neither lie at full length nor sit upright [...] the slaves had to be chained, right hand to right leg, left hand to left leg, and attached in rows to long iron bars. In this position they lived for the voyage. [...]
No place on earth, observed one writer of the time, concentrated so much misery as the hold of a slave ship.
Twice a day, at nine and at four, they received their food. To the slave-traders they were articles of trade and no more.«[30]

They were pawns in the infamous Triangular Trade: European ships set sail for the Caribbean colonies with bartering goods, arms, and liquor for African slave traders; slaves were captured and shipped from Africa to the islands; and in the final step, sugar and rum were exported from the Caribbean back to Europe.

The average life expectancy for an imported slave was only seven years, but history tells that many died within the first

---

30 Mintz (1971): op. cit., pp. 7-8

year after they arrived. The acclimatizing period, or *seasoning* as it was called, was a time of brutal adjustment for the new slaves. They were forced to adopt new cultural customs and languages. On the plantations, owners demanded slaves sever every tie to their homelands and kept slaves of the same culture apart; rebellion was still common. They exercised harsh punishments for disobedience or acts of will; indeed, it was not illegal to kill an African man in the British colonies until the beginning of the 19th century.

In the 1770s, anti-slavery movements began to take shape in Europe. The Society for the Abolition of Slavery was established in 1787 to raise public awareness of the inhumane treatment of slaves. It was not until 1807, however, that a law was passed banning the trade of slaves on British ships. Soon after the law was passed, many other countries enacted similar laws; in 1831, a massive anti-slavery rebellion in Jamaica destroyed many sugar estates, motivating Parliament to sanction the Emancipation Act of 1834. After a four-year »apprenticeship« during which the slaves were still bound to plantation life, they were released unconditionally.

Cuba was still importing slaves until 1865, and did not officially abolish slavery until 1888. The French possessions did not free their slaves until 1848, followed by the Dutch in 1863 and Puerto Rico in 1873. Many freed slaves purchased parcels of land for subsistence farming. On some of the smaller Caribbean islands, however, there was little land left to buy, so they had to return to plantation work. With the single exception of Haiti (the former French colony of Saint Domingue on Hispaniola) - which was the first Caribbean nation to gain independence from European powers when in 1791 a slave rebellion of the black Jacobins led by Toussaint L'Ouverture started the Haitian Revolution establishing Haiti as a free, black republic by 1804 - all the islands remained colonies until the twentieth century. Many of them changed hands frequently. Spain, the first colonizer, lost much of her Empire to England and France in the seventeenth and eighteenth century, and the remainder to the United States at the end of the nineteenth century. Within a lapse of time of more than two centuries (ranging from Haiti as first in 1804 to St. Kitts-Nevis as the last in 1983) each island of the Archipelago achieved its independence – Antigua in 1981, the Bahamas in 1973, Barbados 1966, Cuba 1902, Belize 1981, Dominica 1978, the Dominican Republic 1865, Grenada 1974, Guyana 1966, Jamaica 1962, St Lucia 1977, St. Vincent and the Grenadines in 1979, Suriname 1975, Trinidad and Tobago 1962.

Despite that Slavery was firstly an economic manoeuvre, determined by the continuous demand of labour force, it has left behind indelible traces in the memory of the individuals of disparate origins and of entire populations, and its vestiges and repercussions were central in the process of foreign society and culture in the New World. On this regard Mintz asserts that:

»Viewed in terms of transoceanic travel during the seventeenth, eighteenth and nineteenth centuries, and remembering that this was a forced migration, the Atlantic slave trade may well have been the most colossal demographic event of modern times. […]
But if the Atlantic slave trade was significant as a demographic phenomenon, the institution of slavery itself was far more so, as social and cultural phenomenon. The cultural history of the New World had begun to change from the moment of Columbus' first landfall. Thereafter, the New World was viewed by Europeans by a gigantic frontier area into which vast numbers of people from the Old World could pour, seeking their fortunes, escaping the confines of European institutions and European societies, and remaking their lives. In this process, the fates and social histories of the peoples of African origin were to be set apart- often largely and completely, in other cases less extremely- from those of the other newcomers. And, of course, the fates and social histories of the indigenous peoples of the New World, the Native Americans, whose Ancestors had been the real discoverers of the Americas, would differ as well, and depressingly so from those of the European newcomers.«[31]

The Antilles embraces a wide range of local codes of race relations as a result of the peculiarity of the Caribbean social history. The Caribbean islands, in fact, have been and are still settings in which peoples of very different »pasts« but fairly similar »presents« jostled together in new settings with cultural accompaniments of heterogeneity and diversity as a consequence.

---

31 Mintz, Sidney, W. (1989): »Caribbean Transformations«, Columbia University Press, New York, p. 61

By the turn of the past century a black- raced mixed middle stratum emerged and increased gradually in the Caribbean colonies, which is one of the most important social and consequently cultural developments after the end of slavery. Furthermore the post- slavery immigration seeking for labour made the Caribbean region more ethnically and culturally diverse. This meant that Caribbean societies were becoming more complex.

»The process of 'creolization'- a blending, but also a confrontation of the region's culture, the nature of which has been the subject of a huge debate among and between local residents and foreign scholars- which arguably began on the slave ships themselves, and continued to affect all aspects of plantation society, was now at its most evident, most public as a form of expression.«[32]

Through its history the Caribbean has revealed a great complexity of social relations and the influence of such variables as race, ethnicity, migration and multifaceted dependency (socio-economic condition, popular culture, institutional mimicry) on politics.

Caribbean culture is the result of a syncretism that comes from the relationship among several human groups of different origin and from various types of cultural creativity. According to Mintz, the Caribbean society is a plural society where: »the cultural homogeneity of society (as it existed before western contact) is replaced by a culturally and racially heterogeneous society.«[33]

The various ethnic groups in the Antilles inhabit distinct but complementary cultural spheres, in which the heterogeneous cultural elements have been drawn together because of the dominant political structure of the colonial authority. Although the process of enslavement »africanized« the islands (in fact most of their cultures and peoples are African in origin) Euro-

---

32 Brereton, Bridget/Yeviltgton, Kevin, A. (edited by) (1999): »The colonial Caribbean in Transition, Essays on Postemancipation Social and Cultural«, The Press University of the West Indies, Barbados, Jamaica, Trinidad & Tobago, p. 8
33 Mintz (1971): op.cit., p 97

peans oppressed peoples from diverse part of the Hemisphere. That is to say, that:

»Caribbean history is not only black history, but also yellow history, red history, brown history, and _ not surprisingly _ white history, so far as the testament of oppression is concerned.«[34]

This process is evidently reflected in the social stratification of the population. In almost every island different gradations coexist and interpenetrate, and each aspect of the Caribbean reveals blending and separatism, side by side.

»[...] yet the man of colour who was nearly white despised the man of colour who was only half-white, who in turn despised the man of colour who was only quarter white, and so on through all the shades. [...]
It all reads like a cross between a nightmare and a bad joke. But these distinctions still exercise their influence in the West Indies to-day.«[35]

One of the islands most affected by this creation of a social cultural potpourri of different ethnic groups is Trinidad. The former British colony has been studied for several decades and considered as an emblematic example of plural society, where Africans, Indians, East Indian, Europeans, Chinese and in a smaller number, other kind of ethnic groups cohabit the twin nation of Trinidad and Tobago.

Columbus landed in Trinidad in 1498, and the island was settled by the Spanish a century later. The original inhabitants – Arawaks and Carib Indians – were largely wiped out by the Spanish colonizers, and the survivors were gradually assimilated. Although it attracted the French (who came in large number at the end of the eighteenth century, outnumbering the Spanish population, free Black, and other non-Spanish settlers), Trinidad remained under Spanish rule until the British captured it in 1797.

At that time the island's economy was mainly fuelled by the captive labour brought by French planters from other islands. The French settlers were sufficient in size and capital to assert a strong influence on the economic and political development of

---

34 Mintz (1989): op. cit., p. 49
35 James (1989): op. cit, p. 43

the colony. Additionally, the French culture and language now spoken by the majority of the population, made a strong impact on the culture and on the social life of the island. The white French and Spanish minority formed the pinnacle of the racial pyramid, followed by the free coloured and black settlers, and finally the slaves. As with the other Caribbean colonies, Trinidad was stratified by race and class.

Historically -unfortunately still today- the light skinned is the preferred population. Although colour is often tossed aside as a non-issue, it is something that tends to come up time and time again, the colour complex, the stereotyping of individuals based on skin tone, is deeply embedded in the black consciousness-, the issue of skin colour has been used as a means of controlling and division. Skin colour, in fact, has been used effectively to disrupt unity.

When the British gained the full control of the colony, they had to face the problem of administrating a largely Roman Catholic French speaking population. In order to minimize the very possible consequences of this problem, aggravated also by the presence of a great number of diverse peoples and merging cultures, they established a Crown colony system of government, which was directly ruled by Britain.

The majority of Trinidadians are Indians or have African origins; the enslaved African population (the Africans were imported from 1516 to 1834) came from various cultural, linguistic, and religious backgrounds mainly from West Africa. Groups of free blacks from America and other Caribbean islands also populated Trinidad during and after slavery. During the post- emancipation period, after 1838 when slavery was formally abolished, Trinidad's ethnic composition was further complicated by the indenture of Portuguese and Chinese groups to supply plantation labour. However, these groups were not found suitable for the arduous labour of plantation work and instead became involved in grocery and dry goods trading. After World War II, the Syrians and Lebanese joined the already diverse population growing in Trinidad. Furthermore, the importation of approximately 144,000 indentured labourers from India (from 1838 to 1917) had a profound impact on the demographics of the island's society in comparison to some of the other groups. In addition, a small number of Venezuelans also immigrated to Trinidad during the nineteenth century.

Despite achieving its freedom in 1962 from Great Britain, forming with Tobago the independent and formally unified nation of Trinidad and Tobago, race and class hierarchies, ethnic tension and fragmentation within the population are still realities which the Trinbagonians have to face. Today, Trinidad and Tobago's people are mainly of African or East Indian descent. Virtually all speak English. Small percentages also speak Hindi, French patois, and several other dialects. Trinidad has two major folk traditions: Creole and East Indian. Creole is a *mélange* of African elements with Spanish, French, and English colonial culture. Trinidad's East Indians- who mostly remained on the land, and still dominate the agricultural sector or, more recently, have become prominent in business and the professions- have retained much of their own way of life, including Hindu and Muslim religious festivals and practices. Thus, according to Mintz:

»Although the cultural framework of the Indian and Creole people appears to be fundamentally different, nevertheless there are more values held in common than appears at the first sight. For instance, the acceptance of the British social system and its scale of values as a superior one led to the partial incorporation of a whole series of values and attitudes characteristic of that system. These values and attitudes are more or less incompatible with the culture of the system of values of the subordinate ethnic groups, and a process of gradual shedding of the latter has consequently taken place. Thus, although the ascriptive colour values were the dominant ones in the island, the universalistic-achievement values of the larger social system also invaded the island society. [...] The dominant demands of the subordinate social groups, both lower class Creole and Indian, came to be expressed in this demand of equality for treatment, a demand that was not incompatible with the new goals that the society has come to accept.«[36]

Therefore, Trinidad should be considered as a »plural society«, where a multitude of cultures and traditions interweave to form a »universal« *continuum* built up by unbroken intersections in

---

36 Mintz (1971): op. cit., 1971, p. 108

which the habits of the various communities have intervened in order to »invent« and create a national culture. The result is a hybrid/creole culture, that is, according to Yelvington:

»[...] more secular cultural institutions _ [...] for instance the pre-Lenten Carnival in Trinidad_ also developed and flourished as a creative mélange of African, European and uniquely Caribbean influences. Popular music, song and dance folklore all reflected a similar mélange, and continued to develop despite official disapproval or actual persecution. The process of 'creolization'_ a blending, but also a confrontation of the region's cultures, the nature of which has been the subject of a huge debate amongst and between local resident and foreign scholars_ which arguably began on the slave ships themselves, and continued to affect all aspects of plantation society, was now at its most public as a form of expression.«[37]

In various permutations and combinations cultural developments have a revolutionary impact; therefore cultural representations might be seen as fundamental to the creation of a common history and culture. In a gradual and constant way, after the abolition of slavery, the population took and still consciously take part in the process of dismantling the authority once commanded by the English masters.

As Yevilgton pointed out in the reference mentioned above, Carnival is thus suitable as a model for post-emancipation/ postcolonial representations of the body politic that seek to dismantle the hierarchised corpus of imperial culture, as a medium of the multivoiced or polyphonic spirit which effectively opposes monologic orders such as colonialism.

Caribbean culture is the result of a syncretism that comes from the relationship among several human groups of different origin and from various types of cultural creativity. Secular festivals, like carnival, are derived from pre-colonial traditions which have been altered in response to changing circumstances and contexts. Because of the tendency of being relatively open in structure, these festivals often become highly syncretic events which incorporate many elements of colonising culture even while expressing difference and/or dissent from them.

---

37 Brereton/Yevilgton: op. cit, p. 8

Most of these secular festivals are rooted in cyclical and calendar rituals in which the whole collective participates. At certain moments of the seasonal cycle, which are defined differently in various cultures, certain groups or categories of people usually occupying inferior positions exercise ritual authority over their superiors, by establishing a hierarchy that resembles a parody of the normal hierarchical order of their superiors.

The political dimension of the ritual intersects with the sacred, not least because many rituals were officially banned by imperial agents. Such forbidden events became subversive activities under colonial rule and can now function as symbols of liberty and national culture for an independent and unified post-colonial system, especially when ritual is contextualized by or located in a particular community. Indeed, according to Luigi Sampietro:

»The Caribbean muse is hybrid, composite and elusive […], yet sturdy muse of a composite protean polyglot art […] whose quest any one of us can identify spontaneously at the symbolic level. This is why the literature (cultural representations*) she inspires speaks to us all.«[38]

---

* My addition. In this context Sampietro's assumption could be also referred to all the cultural representations of the Caribbean area, rather than just to the literary production.

38 Sampietro, Luigi: »The Specificity of Caribbean Literature«, in Sampietro, Luigi (edited by) (1991): »Caribana«, Vol. 2, Bulzoni Editore, Roma, p. 11

III. Gender and Post-Colonialism

Pandora's Daughters: Origins of Women's Subordination

»The famous lame smith took clay and, through Zeus's counsels,
gave it the shape of a modest maiden.
Athena, the grey eyed goddess, clothed her and decked her out
with a flashy garment and then with her hands
she hung over her head a fine draping veil, a marvel to behold;
Pallas Athena crowned her head with lovely wreaths
of fresh flowers that had just bloomed in the green meadows.
The famous lame smith placed on her head a crown of gold
Fashioned by the skill of his own hands
To please the heart of Zeus father.
It was a wondrous thing with many intricate designs
of all the dreaded beasts nurtured by land and sea.
Such grace he breathed into the many marvels therein
that they seemed endowed with life and voice.
Once he had finished- not something good but a mixture
of good and bad- he took the maiden before gods and men,
and she delighted in the finery given her by gray- eyed Athena,
daughter of a mighty father. Immortal gods and mortal men,
were amazed when they saw this tempting snare
from which men cannot escape. From her comes the fair sex;
yes, wicked womenfolk are her descendants.
They live among mortal men as a nagging burden
and are no good sharers of abject want, but only of wealth.[...]
So too, Zeus who roars on high made the women
to be an evil for mortal men, helpmates in deeds of harshness.
And he bestowed another gift, evil in place of good:
whoever does not wish to marry, fleeing the malice of women,
reaches harsh old age with none to care for him;
then even if he is well provided,
he dies at the end only to have his livelihood shared
by distant kin. And even the man who does marry
and has a wife of sound and prudent mind
spends his life ever trying to balance the bad
and the good in her. But he who marries into a foul brood

> lives plagued by unabating trouble in his heart
> and his mind, and there is no cure for his plight.«
> (Hesiod, Theogony, 561-612)

If any human society- whether in the past or nowadays, large or small, in the West, East or South, First or Third World- is to survive, it must have a sample of social life that comes to the terms with the differences between sexes. In every known society the individuals have elaborated the biological division of labour into forms which most of the times are remotely and fully related to the original biological differences that provided the fundamental clues and this assignment has always been arbitrary.

The notion of femininity and masculinity, and of sexuality are embraced in the concept of gender, which is produced by social practices of knowledge representation, and social practices are so adept at engendering differently gendered subjectivities that their cultural construction becomes invisible, and the final assemblage appears entirely 'natural'.

Gender is a linguistic artefact, a theoretical concept, a feminist invention, a quasi-object shaped in order to deal with bodies, sexualities, the desire, power, and the politics of knowledge, although the popular, as well as intellectual, interpretation of gender was more or less synonymous with 'woman'. According to Judith Butler's explanation of the concept 'gender', it is to say that:

»[...] gender is not to culture as sex is to nature; gender is also the discursive/cultural means by which 'sexed nature' or 'natural sex' is produced and established as 'prediscursive', prior to culture, a politically neutral surface on which culture acts. [...] This production of sex as the prediscursive ought to be understood as the effect of the apparatus of cultural construction designated by gender.«[39]

Although it is ascertained that the nature of women and men are different and specific, and this sexual differentiation bears both the eternal finality of nature and the inexorable inevitabil-

---

[39] Butler, Judith (1999): »Gender troubles, Feminism and the Subversion of Identity«, Routledge, New york and London, p. 11

ity of evolution, society requires and utilizes both the difference itself and the specific skills of each sex. The sexual division of labour is thus doubly determined: by nature, through the biological nature of women and men and the progressive differentiation thereof, and by society, through the social functions these natures and these differences serve. On this concern, Margaret Mead in her famous book »Male and Female«, rhetorically asked herself:

»Do real differences exist, in addition to the obvious anatomical and physical ones- but just biologically based- that may be masked by the learnings appropriated to any given society, but which will nevertheless be there? Will such differences run through all of men's and women's behaviour? Must we expect, for instance, that a brave girl may be very brave but will never have the same kind of courage as a brave boy, and that the man who works all day at a monotonous task may learn to produce far more than any woman in his society, but he will do it at a higher price to himself? Are such differences, and must we take them into account?«[40]

In order to question women's subordination, indeed, it should be challenged between different discourses of sexuality and socio/cultural constructions of femininity.

In the mythical imagination, more often than not, woman is an afterthought, created as a secondary category following the prior emergence of man. In the Greek mythology the first woman was pictured as a wonderful being, a mixture contrasted between beauty, grace, cleverness and malice, and a high and dangerous/seductive power. She was *kalon kakòn*, the beautiful evil, the fatal seductress par excellence, the image of the woman herself, in whom is mirrored the fate of the human being in the hands of its own craft, who was ambivalently called *Pandora* by Hermes (from *didomi*= to donate, because ironically she received gifts from all the gods and, at the same time, she was blessed by Zeus with the features of a desirable, wonderful and luminous bride). Her presence on earth is the

---

40 Mead, Margaret (1970): »Male and Female, A Study of the Sexes in a Changing World«, William Morrow & Company, New York, p. 8

punishment planed by Zeus himself for Prometeo's disobedience, in order to remind the men the unbridgeable gap between mortal and immortal.

Pandora is the personification of man's ambiguous structural position between divinity and bestiality. In order to persist through time, the man must continuously reconstitute himself through reproduction and ritual, since he is no longer immortal and constant as the divinities; she is, indeed, the deceit gift par excellence, for without her man cannot reproduce himself. Pandora's daughters are, consequently, the women, all the women, and not only according to Greek mythology. It is true that Pandora is a mythological figure, therefore not necessarily a literary character which suddenly emanated from man's imagination. Already in the classical age there was the conviction that the *mythos* has a strong rational »pigmentation«. In Plato's Phaedro, Socrates seems willing to demonstrate that the myth is nothing but the imaginative covering of a real fact (natural/human aspect). On this point, Silvia Gherardi by explaining the invalidity of the neutral and neuter nature of organizations and the fact that they are structured according to the symbolism of gender, asserts that:

»The hypothetical story of the birth of civil society displays a manifest paradox. It claims to be based on universal freedom, but simultaneously denies this attribute to women. [...]
It is found not only in the Greek myths, in the struggles between the deities of the first and second generation, but also in other cosmogonies. The features common to these narratives is that they omit to mention that the sons did not subvert the patriarchal order to establish universal civil liberty, but to get the women for themselves. [...] The original contract envisaged both the freedom of men and the subjection of women.
The paradox is this: if women do not enjoy natural freedom they cannot be subject to a contract, nor can they possess the characteristics of an 'individual'. Moreover, the opposition between the state of nature and civil society creates a further paradox: between public and private, between public-man and private woman.«[41]

---

41 Gherardi, Silvia (1995): »Gender, Symbolism and Organizational Cultures«, SAGE Publications, London, New Delhi, Thousand Oaks, p. 41

Throughout history women have not been defined as beings in their own right, but in terms of how they stand in relation to men -for example, as emotional rather than rational, as physically weaker, or as domestically rather than publicly oriented. In this process women have been designated »the second sex«, that is, secondary to men. Therefore the analysis of culture and its diverse aspects has a great importance for its function of allowing links made between organizational process and individual identity, enabling us to explore the complexity of identity and the factors which influence the patterns of differentiation within an organization. In this light the issue of women's representations may be examined as an effect, albeit variable, of gender oppression. The anthropologist Margaret Mead was one of the first scholars who pointed out that:

»As a civilisation becomes complex, human life is defined in individual terms as well as in the service of the race, and the great structures of law and government, religion and art and science, become something highly valued for themselves. Practised by men, they become indicators of masculine humanity, and men take great pride in these achievements. To the extent that women are barred from them, women become less human.«[42]

In the thirties Margaret Mead, in the comparative study of the relationship between sex and character (natural disposition) in diverse societies in New Guinea (the »Seven South Sea Peoples«: the Samoans, the Manus of the Admiralty Islands, the mountain Arapesh, the cannibal Mundugumor of the Yuat River, the lake dwelling Tchambuli, the Iatmul Head hunters of the Great Sepik River, the Balinese), clearly understood the cultural and fluctuating nature of the feminine and masculine behaviour and dispositions, which insofar were mostly considered as phylogenetic aspects determined by gendered biological diversities (Eibl-Eibesfeldt 1997).

Throughout history, for example, the artist's engagement with metaphors, symbols, visual representations and language, offers a significant picture of the universal image of sexuality; most of the times the representation of women may have its

---

42 Mead: op. cit., p. 382

part in a cultural symbolism where they are not representers and do not possess knowledge. That is to say, indeed, that they have always been seen as (paraphrasing Levì Strauss) the objects not the agents, and as means of communication, not themselves communicator.

In this society, where the division of mind and matter has been necessary for distinguishing the human control over the natural world and the man/animal differentiation, the cultural representations of a woman as a whore to a woman as an angel has been paralleled by the development of this process, that is the pursuit of rationality and consequentially the appropriation of nature.

The mind/matter and man/nature-animal generated contradictory representations of women as sexually inert, innocent and holy, object of artistic inspiration, and, on the other hand, ignorant, potentially bestial, subjected to the social/men's control (aimed to the procreation). For example, in the *dolce stil novo* the woman's beauty is drawn as the symbol of God's beauty, by which the soul *(anima)* is inspired. But the poet's ecstasy and the joy of contemplation is tempted by the sordid resistance to the passions, whose instigator is performed by women, and where the human love is morally and consciously justified by its intrinsic relationship with the holy love. Dante, in one of his most famous sonnets collected in the vita nova, gave a wonderful explanation of these human struggles, and description of the poetic metaphor of woman/angel.

»Tanto gentile e tanto onesta pare
la donna mia, quand' ella altrui saluta,
ch' ogne lingua deven tremando muta,
e gli occhi no l' ardiscon di guardare.
Ella si va, sentendosi laudare,
benignamente e d'umiltà vestuta;
e par che sia una cosa venuta
dal cielo in terra a miracol mostrare.
Mostrasi sí piacente a chi la mira,
che dà per li occhi una dolcezza al core,
che 'ntender nolla può chi nolla prova.

E par che de la sua labbia si mova un spirito soave pien d'amore,
che va dicendo a l' anima: Sospira.«[43]
(Dante, sonetto xv, Vita Nova)

Beatrice's image in Dante may be seen as the »eternal feminine«, according to the Jungian concept of the Anima archetype, that is, of the spiritual/not-human/irrational guide. Carl Gustav Jung attributes human rational thought to be the male nature, while the irrational aspect is considered to be natural female. Consequently, irrationality is the male anima shadow and rationality is the female animus shadow.

This dualism of the human being brought the necessity of choosing the supremacy of rationality in order to pursue the »perfection«, that is, the sharp distinction between human and animal. Thus, if the model was a model of choice between the two elements, than the women's capacity for rationality had to be less than men's, and then the image of woman as sexually innocent and passionless became not a truth of nature but a social and moral aim, that is, the need of suppressing sexual appetite in order to achieve a fully human existence. In fact, according to Margaret Mead:

»When human beings view their biological inheritance and consider to what extent they are bound by it, women appear at once as the more intractable material. Conception and birth are as stubborn conditions of life as death itself. Coming to terms with the rhythms of women's lives means coming to term with the life itself, accepting the imperatives of

---

[43] So winsome and so worthy seems to me/ my lady, when she greets a passer-by, / that every tongue can only babble shy/ and eager glances lose temerity.
Sweetly and dressed in all humility, /away she walks from all she's praisèd by, /and truly seems a thing come from the sky to show on earth what miracles can be.
So much she pleases every gazing eye, /she gives a sweetness through it to the heart, /which he who does not feel it fails to guess.
A spirit full of love and tenderness / seems from her features ever to depart, /that, reaching for the soul, says softly »Sigh.«

the body rather than the imperatives of an artificial manmade, perhaps transcendentally beautiful society.«[44]

The symbolic associations given by the fact of being man or woman offer a way of linking sexual ideologies and stereotypes both to the wider system of cultural symbols and to social roles or experiences, which are identified with the expectation and values which individual cultures associate with being male or female. Jung called these forms or symbols, manifested by all people in all cultures, archetypes, which are implicit in dreams, visions, myths, legends, fairy tales, and cultural manifestations of all types, and contained in the *collective unconscious*, that is the part of the human unconscious common to all the human beings. Dr Edward Edinger explained the meaning of the Jungian archetype as:

»An archetype is to the psyche what an instinct is to the body [...]
Just as instincts are unknown motivating dynamisms of biological behaviour, archetypes are unknown motivating dynamisms of the psyche. Archetypes are the psychic instincts of the human species.«[45]

In other words this confirms the arbitrary foundation of women's representations. Indeed, it might be that women exist just in relation to men, but only as Fanon's black man exists just in relation to the white man:

»For not only must the black man be black; he must be black in relation to the white man. Some critics will take it on themselves to remind us that the position has a converse. I say that this is false. The black man has no ontological resistance in the eyes of the white man. Overnight the Negro has been given two frames of reference within which he has had to place himself. His metaphysics, or less pretentiously, his customs and the sources on which they were based, were wiped out because they

---

44 Mead: op.cit., p. 181
45 Edinger, Edward (1968): »An Outline of Analytical Psychology«, Quadrant, pp. 1-11, quoted by Knapp, Bettina, L. (1987): »Women in Twentieth-Century Literature: A Jungian View«, Pennsylvania State University Press, University Park, p. 3

were in conflict with a civilization that he did not know and that imposed itself on him.«[46]

Therefore, according to Margaret Mead:

»Women, it is truth, make human beings, but only men can make men. [...]
But if whole societies can build their ceremonials upon an envy of women's role and desire to imitate it, than it should be easier to explore the possibility that envy of the other sex, or doubt of the authenticity of the other sex, is a possibility of the life history of both sexes, a possibility that may be immensely fostered by cultural arrangements, but which is always present.«[47]

Cultural representations, indeed, underpin the hierarchy of female roles in the traditional structure of the society.
In fact, according to Margaret Mead:

»In every known human society the male's need for achievement can be recognised. Man may cook, or weave or dress dolls or hunt humming birds, but if such activities are appropriate occupations of men, then the whole society, men and women alike, votes them as important. When the same occupations are performed by women, they are regarded as less important. In a great number of human societies men's sureness of their sex role is tied up with their right, or ability, to practise some activity that women are not allowed to practise. Their maleness, in fact, has to be underwritten by preventing women from entering some field or performing some feat. [...]
There seems no evidence that it is necessary for men to surpass women in any specific way, but rather that men do need to find a reassurance in achievement, and because of this connection, cultures frequently phrase achievement as something that women do or cannot do, rather than directly as something which men do well. [...]
In the case of women, it is only necessary that they be permitted by the given of social arrangements to fulfil their biological role, to attain this sense of irreversible achievement.«[48]

---

46 Fanon (1986): op. cit., p. 110
47 Mead: op. cit., pp. 103-104
48 Ibid, pp. 159-60

But these cultural constructions have themselves been the target of change, and these social divisions are being realigned in intricate ways. In complex societies of today, with the spread of the dual presence into almost all societal areas, social differentiation is articulated and enmeshed with other dimensions (for example class and gender). The evolution process of a society, whereby customs considered natural are no longer acceptable, is also changing the classic social distinction of gender.

Culture is depicted in terms of »shared values« and as the site of a common consensus, in which norms and values are normally deeply embedded. Thus, although culture has often been wanted and pictured as static, the dynamics of the organizational politics and social realities, the production of new values, norms and visions provoke the manipulation of symbols and consequently the mobilization of traditional norms and values. Cultural change becomes a source of potential conflicts and division as well as consensus.

Nowadays it is increasingly difficult in democratic societies to come up with moral justification for gender as a social destiny; consequently emancipation, liberation and repression are much more closely interwoven than mutually exclusive.

A Double Colonization

»I am white: that is to say that I possess beauty and virtue, which have never been black. I am the colour of the daylight. [...]
I am black: I am the incarnation of a complete fusion with the world, an intuitive understanding with the earth, an abandonment with my ego in the heart of cosmos, and no white man, no matter how intelligent he may be, can ever understand Louis Armstrong and the music of the Congo.
[...] I am truly a ray of sunlight under the earth. [...]
And there one lies body to body with one's blackness or one's whiteness, in full narcissistic cry, each sealed into his own peculiarity- with, it is true, now and then a flash or so, but these are threatened at theirsource
From the first this is how the problem appears to Mayotte- at the fifth year of her age and the third page of her book: »She took the inkwell out of the desk and emptied over his head«. This was her own way of turning whites into blacks [...] and there were Loulouze and her mother, who told her that life was difficult for a woman of colour. So, since she could

> no longer try to blacken, to negrify the world, she was going to try, in her own body and in her own mind, to bleach it.«[49]
> (Frantz Fanon, Black Skin White Masks)

In various permutations and combinations cultural developments have a revolutionary impact on different disciplines and consequently these developments cannot be considered in isolation from the growth of certain political movements such as feminism or anti-colonial struggles, mainly for the reasons that both women and colonised peoples functioned in economies which rested on their labour, and both were subject to ideologies which justified this exploitation. Indeed, feminism, as well as the anti-colonial movement, are of crucial interest to post-colonial discourse, since they have often been concerned with the ways and extents to which culture and its representations are fundamental to identity formation and the construction of subjectivity. In other words:

»Feminist, and post-colonial discourses both seek to reinstate the marginalized in the face of the dominant, and early feminist theory, like early nationalist post-colonial criticism, was concerned with inverting the structures of domination, substituting, for instance a female tradition or traditions for a male dominated canon.«[50]

Thus, Postcolonial studies address important concerns such as the impact of colonial practices on the production and representation of identities, the relationship between global capital and power, and the relevance of gender, race, and class for understanding domination and resistance.

The process of forming an identity is often strictly connected with the idea of belonging to a common nation, an imagined community which have to be endowed with a historical, racial and cultural unity. Anti-colonial struggles therefore had to create new and powerful identities for colonised peoples in order to challenge colonialism at political, cultural and emotional levels. In these particular circumstances the idea of the nation was

---

49 Fanon (1986): op. cit., p.45
50 Ashcroft/Griffiths/Tiffin (2004): op. cit., p. 249

a great vehicle for harnessing anti-colonial energies at all these levels.

Very often national fantasies, be they colonial, anti-colonial or postcolonial, played also with the connection between women, land or nations. In fact, if the nation is an imagined community, that imagining is profoundly gendered. For instance, across the colonial spectrum, the nation-state or its guiding principles are often imagined literally as a woman. The female figure symbolises the nation which is metaphorically pictured as a mother which embraces and protects her children, that is the population.

The deployment of gendered symbols in the construction of collective identities, in particular of national entities and the legitimisation of states, are central to the construction of the boundaries of state and nationhood. As national emblems, women are usually cast as mother or wives, and are called upon to literally and figuratively reproduce the nation, by representing an ancestral and fixed tradition. Colonialism intensified patriarchal relations in colonised lands, often because native men, increasingly disenfranchised and excluded from the public sphere, became more tyrannical at home. They seized upon the home and the woman as emblems of their culture and nation.

As mothers to the nation, women are granted limited agency. Arguments for women's education in metropolitan as well as colonial contexts rely on the logic that instruction will make them better wives and mothers. At the same time educated women have to be taught not to overstep their boundaries and usurp authority from men. Colonising as well as anti-colonising men, while being otherwise opposed, have often shared certain attitudes to women; in this term black or/and colonised women have endured a double colonisation whose consequences are still today so manifest. Thus, when races, classes, sexes, and nations are viewed as distinct cultural constructions, existing in determinate relations within distinct structures, then the questions of cause, effect and intervention can be posed within a new problem, where inequality is social and contingent, not natural and necessary.

Both feminists and colonised peoples, like other subordinate groups, have used appropriation to subvert and adapt dominant culture and its signifying practices. Postcolonial women writers cover a range of issues that share a concern with gender, for example, how their female protagonist's self and sexuality are constructed and controlled by indigenous patriarchies and colonial practices.

Women, as women, are subject to patriarchal structures and sexist, misogynist cultures. This is true of all women, in all places: partnered women and single women; women with children, women without children; women with salaried work, women with unpaid/domestic work, and women who have both; women in dominant races/cultures, women in subordinate races/cultures; women in industrial colonialist societies and women in underdeveloped colonized societies. But, according to Victoria Ana Goddard, if it is true that:

»Because gender identities are integral to the construction of subjectivity and to the placing of individuals in their social world, they are central to broader issues of identity and inform discourses pertaining to the social universe, to change, community and nationhood. Gender categorisations cut across divisions in terms of class, ethnicity and community, and are located in the interstices of institutional and individual practices and ideologies.«[51]

It is also certain that the image of a greater uniformity among the women of different areas of the world is probably somewhat illusory. In fact, as Chandra Mohanty points out:

»There is, however, a particular world balance of power within which any analysis of culture, ideology and socio-economic conditions has to be necessarily situated. [...]
Western feminist scholarship cannot avoid the challenge of situating itself and examining its role in such a global economic and political framework. To do any less would be to ignore the complex interconnections between first- and third- world economies and the profound effect of this on the lives of women in all countries.«[52]

---

51 Goddard, Victoria, Ana (2000): »Gender, Agency, and Change: Anthropological Perspectives«, Routledge, New York and London, p. 2
52 Chandra, Talpade, Mohanty: »Under Western Eyes: Feminist Scholarship and Colonial Discourses«, in Williams, Patrick/ Chrisman Laura (edited by) (1994): »Colonial Discourse and

In other words, she stresses the fact that:

»An analysis of 'sexual difference' in a form of cross-culturally singular monolithic notion of patriarchy or male dominance leads to the construction of a similarly reductive and homogeneous notion of what I shall call the 'third world difference'- that stable, ahistorical something that apparently oppresses most if not all the women in this country.«[53]

Evidence of gaps between regions and groups undermine proclamations of a homogenised feminism, therefore its universality might be challenged. In the 1980s, many feminist critics (Carby 1982; Mohanty 1984; Suleri 1992), began to bring to light the fact that Western feminism was operating from hidden, universalistic assumptions with a middle-class, Euro-centric preconception. They demonstrated how the peculiarity of the strategy between First and Third World women lead to very different perceptions of the nature of political struggle and priorities. That is to say, as Kirsten Holst Petersen questions- after having listened to a speech of a group of German feminists during a conference on »The Role of Women in Africa«-, that:

»One obvious and very important area of difference is this: whereas Western feminists discuss the relative importance of feminist versus class emancipation, the African discussion is between feminist emancipation versus the fight against neo-colonialism, particularly in its cultural aspects. In other words: which is the more important, which comes first, the fight for female equality or the fight against Western cultural imperialism?«[54]

Moreover, Gayatri Spivak demonstrates the relativism of western feminism assumptions by assuming that a piece of writing or politics concerning emancipation/liberation aspects and referring to one specific contest, may act as a colonizing agent when referred to in another contest.

    Postcolonial Theory«, Pearson Education, Harlow Essex England, p 198
53 Ibid.
54 Petersen, Holst, Kirsten: »First Things First: Problems of a Feminist Approach to African Literature«, in Ashcroft/ Griffiths/ Tiffin (2004): op. cit, pp. 251-52

In the majority of past colonial echoes and the present post-/ neo-colonial conditions, Third World women are identified, indeed, with the anti-imperialist and wage struggles rather than with the images and dominant preoccupations of First World feminism. Thus, in this process, the protagonists of the various movements of emancipation should not be homogenized in order to achieve a deep and well constructed analysis of the principal aims given by the diversity of the places, religions, sexual and politic orientation and colour.

In the past decades, Third World feminism has been concerned that categories like gender may sometimes be ignored within the larger formation of the colonial and that postcolonial theory has tended to elide gender differences in constructing a single category of the colonized, although there are similarities between the proprieties and strategies actuated by third world feminist and post-colonial theory and practice- in the sense that they have often been concerned with the ways and extent to which cultural phenomena and representations are crucial to identity formation and to the construction of subjectivity-.

For both groups, culture has been a vehicle for subverting patriarchal and imperial power and both discourses have invoked essentialist arguments in positing more authentic forms of cultural productions against those imposed on them. Both discourses share a sense of disarticulation from an inherited culture and have thus attempted to recover an authenticity via pre-colonial traditions. However, these critics argue that colonialism operated very differently for women and for men and that women were subject both to general discrimination as colonial subjects and specific discrimination as women needs to be taken into account, Gayatri Spivak points out:

»Within the effaced itinerary of the subaltern subject, the track of sexual difference is doubly affected. The question is not of female participation in insurgency, or the ground rules of the sexual division of labour, for both of which there is 'evidence'. It is, rather, that, both as object of colonialist historiography and as subject of insurgency, the ideological construction of gender keeps the male dominant. If, in the contest of colonial production, the subaltern has no history and cannot speak, the subaltern as female is even more deeply in shadow [...].«[55]

Consequently, Ania Loomba, in her essay »Colonialism/Postcolonialism«, asserts that:

»Non white feminists have written alternative histories of women's oppression, and also offered alternative blueprints for action.«[56]

Therefore women share specific gender concerns in terms of how social and cultural factors appear from a female point of view, often by exploring imaginatively several conflicts between tradition and modernisation, as well as by bringing back the complex oral traditions that have undergone varieties of transformations through colonial print-dominated tendency. In other words »postcolonial women« speak from a multiple and complex social, historical and cultural positionality which constitutes the female subjectivity.

According to Mikhail Bakhtin, he questioned the function of the language as an expression of social identity and consequently as a medium of consciousness; that is to say, that if this theory is related to cultural phenomena and representation, than postcolonial women share a range of issues that concern not just the relationship with the »Other«, but as well an internal dialogue with the plural aspects of otherness within the self.

Postcolonial women writers, for instance, explore their personal dimensions of history, finding inspiration in their own indigenous oral and folk tradition and in the use of literary traditions of ancient/oral languages, by narrowing their daily experiences within a patriarchal and former colonial society and, by so doing, they represent the personal (intimacy) as a political act through their literary texts. Thus, despite geographic and cultural differences, these »Subalterns between Subalterns« give voice to »feminized cultural representation«, to marginalised/or black women too often considered as a narrative/socio-

---

55 Spivak, Gayatri, Chacrovorty: »Can the Subaltern Speak?«, in Ashcroft/Griffiths/Tiffin (2004): op. cit., p. 28
56 Loomba, Ania (1998): »Colonialism/Postcolonialism«, Routledge, New York and London, p. 165

cultural object, as victims of a double colonisation and its consequences, by using an hybrid representative and symbolic »frame« (action, strategy) based on the harmonious alternation of diverse modes of cultural productions (where the most common is the writing) languages and traditions. In the actual global panorama of the world, these polyphonic/ multicultural voices gives voice to the deafening silence of their past and present with the aim of dismantling the hegemonic boundaries and the determinants that create unequal relations of power based on binary oppositions such as »us/them«, »first world/third world«, »white/black«, »male/female«, »active/passive« and allowing debates and negotiations.

From Another Point of View: Women of the Caribbean

> »After dat, we kept on meeting – doing drama and talking out about our life experiences. We bout how employers treat helpers. Di lickle bit a pay and di round di clock work. One a di women in a di group tell us about a women who use to give her helper a special tinnin plate and condense can to eat and drink out of. Yuh couldn't eat until the employer finish eating. Di dinner always leave into di pot. Di employer used to tek out di meat, slice it and count out di finger of banana to leave for di helper to eat before she go to work.
>
> Plenty women used to talk bout di children dat we have and ti babyfaada problem. At first, me was shy to talk bout myself. Di impression woman always give me is dat dem is a set of people who always lap dem tail, tek yuh name spread table cloth. Me did feel sort a funny at di time, having children fi two different man, especially since me never like Archie. Me never discuss it wid nobody. When me come meet Didi and hear she talk bout her baby faada and how she hate him after she get pregnant, me say, 'Well if yuh can say your own me can say mine, for we actually deh pon di same ting.' Me and she start talk bout it.
>
> Tings develop so-till we start meet more people and talk bout woman and work and woman and politics. We discuss what is politics and how it affect woman. After we done talk ah get to feel dat di little day-to-day tings dat to we as women, is politics too. For instance, if yuh

tek yuh pickney to hospital and it die in yuh hand- dat is politics. If yuh to yuh own child dat damage him or her fi di future, dat is politics too. If yuh man box yuh down, dat is politics. But plenty politicians don't tink dose tings have anyting to do wid politics.«[57]
(Foxy and Di Macca, Place Work)

Caribbean women have lived in the borderlands of history and society for a long time; until very recently they were defined by their relationship to men, in spite of their daily life, their various ways of resistance, of understanding and changing the world, which have been always devalued and considered insignificant. They have been invisible, unvoiced in the conventional history records, they have experienced –and the great majority is still experiencing- the »alienation within the alienation«, as used by Kenneth Ramchand to picture the choked struggles of Caribbean women. Therefore, according to Bridget Brereton:

»The exclusion of women from conventional history thus reflected systems of gender oppression and in turn reinforced them by encouraging the definition of women as 'Other', the passive, there but not there, never the makers and movers of history.«[58]

Although there are structural similarities in the historical evolution and in the contemporary economic development (particularly in the involvement with the United States), and in the geographical location between the Caribbean and South America, several aspects of both countries have to be treated separately and, for instance, features regarding gender relations, representations, and ideology are just a few of them. Gender is used as the principal and often unique analytical frame for the examination of the multiple and contradictory realities of Caribbean women's lives. By defining the nature of gender system and relations, Eudine Barriteau asserts that:

---

[57] Sistren/Ford-Smith, Honor (edited by) (1986): »Lionhaert Gal, Life stories of Jamaican Women«, The Women's Press Limited, London, pp. 252-53

[58] Brereton, Bridget: »General Problems and Issues in Studying the History of Women«, in Mohamed, Patricia/Shepherd, Catherine (edited by) (1999): »Gender and Caribbean Development«, University of the Wet Indies, Canoe Press,Kingston, Jamaica, p. 120

»Gender relations constitute the continuous social, political, economic, cultural, and psychological expressions of the material and ideological aspects of a gender system. Gender relations encode and sometimes mask unequal power relations between women and men and between women and the state.«[59]

In considering gender relations in the Caribbean, an ample range of factors have to be taken into account, that is, for example, race, class and colour, which have shaped and ordered the Caribbean dominance system and society throughout the Caribbean's past and recent history. Throughout the colonization and the slavery period, Caribbean women suffered most under existing capitalist, patriarchal, white-supremacist social relations and low-income labour. Concerning gender relations, slavery might be seen as a constant changing system of socio-sexual »abuse« of women, based on a pure capitalistic division of labour, which facilitated firstly a dismantlement and then a revolutionary restructuring of traditional African, European and native gender representations while producing unique features of their own. According to Hilary McD Blekes:

»The absurd question has also been asked whether Caribbean slavery was in effect gender blind or gender neutral.«[60]

From the 16th till the 19th century the majority of the slaves imported from West Africa were women. This preference for women slaves was mainly dictated by the necessity of promoting the natural reproduction of the labour force. During the slave period the differences in the division of the labour be-

---

59 Barriteau, Eudine: »Theorizing the Shift from 'Woman' to 'Gender' in Caribbean Feminist Discourse: The Power Relations of Creating Knowledge«, in Barriteau Eudine (edited by) (2003): »Confronting Power, Theorizing Gender: Interdisciplinary Perspectives in the Caribbean«, University Press of the West Indies, Kingston, Jamaica, p. 30
60 McD Beckles, Hilary: »Gender Paradigms in the Social History of Caribbean Slavery«, in Campbell, Carl/Higman, B., W./Moore, Brian, L. (edited by) (2001): »Slavery, Freedom and Gender: The Dynamics of Caribbean Society«, University of the West Indies Press, Barbados, p. 198

tween the sexes were levelled; the various tasks were shared out equally between man and woman, the working conditions under the colonial yoke were for women as hard as they were for men. On this regard Beckles asserts that:

»Enslaved women, then, did not experience any significant preferential mitigating treatment with respect to the legal provisions. For most of the period there was no policy that distinguished enslaved women as deserving of a less harsh condition, partly because they were not conceptually represented, unlike white women, as a gentler, more delicate sex. [...]
Equality in work and under the whip was the operating principle. When adjustments were made by way of social reforms that targeted enslaved women there were always clear economic objectives in mind. This was very much the case when an effort was made after the 1770s to encourage a higher birth rate as it seemed clear to slave-owners that the slave trade from Africa would soon be abolished.«[61]

In addition and as a consequence of this strategy of measuring the human worth purely in labour terms, the social and institutional infrastructures were dismantled:

»Different tribal groups with divergent traditions also found themselves side by side in these alien Caribbean lands, where even the use of their own names was not allowed. The language and religious practices of the slaves were also forbidden. This Caribbean contest provided fertile ground for the reordering of gender relations among the slaves. The process was to continue into post-slavery Caribbean society.«[62]

During the New World slavery, gender identities and attitudes legitimised by the West African tradition were erased and reconfigured and newly contextualised in the Caribbean dimension; in fact, in most of the West African societies the asset of labour ideologies and organization were based on gendered divisions of work and power (for instance on early West Indian

---

61 McD Beckles, Hilary: »Perfect Propety, Enslaved Black Women in the Caribbean«, in Barriteau (2003): op. cit, p. 145
62 Wiltshire-Brodber, Rosina: »Gender, Race and Class«, in Mohammed/ Shepherd: op. cit., p. 137

plantations enslaved men were the majority and they were forced into working activities- like agricultural labour- considered in their tradition as »Women work«). That is to say, according to Beckles:

»While, therefore, the political economy of gender determined the general nature of demand for labour and informed the experiences of the enslaved, the superordinate role of racism shaped colonial representations of Africans and defined them as a culturally inferior and hence worthy of enslavement. The ideology of race, particularly its phenotypic expressions of colour and culture, was less flexible than gender in determining the experiences of enslaved Africans. Social and economic functions considered fit for Africans were not allocated on the basis of gender.«[63]

Therefore, as Rosina Wiltshire-Brodber pointed out, Caribbean gender relations during the slavery:

»[...] were thus relations in flux. They were influenced by a complex interplay of forces in a hierarchy built on race and class.«[64]

By considering the ethnic and cultural heritage of Caribbean people, African and East Indian women need to be analysed separately. Firstly, East Indians were allowed to maintain their languages, religions and cultural traditions, with the result that their social structure of the gender relations »exported« from India was not so pressured as was that of Africans under slavery. Secondly, the majority of East Indian women arrived in the West Indies voluntarily as indentured labourers, leaving their families in the homeland in order to escape from the rigid caste system and patriarchal Indian society and to find equality and »freedom« only in the level of oppression which characterized the indentured labour scheme.

After the 1880s, especially in Trinidad and Guyana- the two islands with a numerous East Indian population- a great num-

---

[63] McD Beckles, Hilary: »Perfect Property, Enslaved Black Women in the Caribbean«, in Barriteau (2003): op. cit, p. 145

[64] Wiltshire-Brodber, Rosina: »Gender, Race and Class«, in Mohammed/ Shepherd: op. cit. p. 138

ber of the East Indians left the estates and established new villages and rural communities as independent peasant farmers. This shift involved the gradual exclusion of Indo-Caribbean women from the »peasant production« to their relegation in a peasant household and in a village life. Indo-Caribbean women, indeed, for the reasons listed above, still remained close to the male dominant model characteristic of traditional Indian society and would have not been particularly representative of Indian women.

The organizational logic of empire, established as a function of white patriarchy, produced a complex framework for the ideological representation of gender, especially black men and women. The control of slaves required it. The survival of colonialism mandated it. Throughout the post-independent period, the industrialisation of the regions required a considerable mass of skilled and unskilled, cheap and easy to manipulate workers; for the fact that, since slavery, Caribbean women have always been on the labour market, they outnumbered men in unskilled work, their wages were lower than the men's, this capitalist manoeuvre was translated into women workers. Moreover liberalism allowed equal participation for men and women in the public once the state created the access, which in reality has never happened.

On the other hand, liberal ideologies shaped the asset of the Caribbean family, by preserving for women the family's realm- that is child bearing, house keeping etc- while excluding them from all the dynamics of household decision-making. The hierarchical structure set in the family was valid and firmly maintained as well in the public sphere, which means that Caribbean women were considered as inferior and second to the men in remuneration, work value and quality, and had less chance in reaching the competences for skilled works and high positions. That is to say, according to Eudine Barritteau:

»The post-independent Caribbean state has gradually opened up the public for women. The state attempts and successfully manipulates and alters material relations of gender while attempting to ignore, or hold constant, the ideological relations of gender. The state alters material relations of gender since these affect the market and, therefore, economic growth and development as defined by its model of development- the

modernization paradigm. States seek to maintain ideological relations of gender as they are.
They assume these relations operate primarily in the private sphere and therefore benefit maintaining the status quo or the structures of the domestic life.«[65]

Indeed, the labour market conditions of women and their representations inherited from the colonial managerial and ideological system, found their continuum in the modern constitution of asymmetric gender relation, creating deep contradictions between the roles performed and expected to be performed by Caribbean women in the public and private sphere.

The position of Caribbean women, especially those of African descent and belonging to the rural class, is, in fact, clearly ambivalent. On one hand they are economically independent and heads of the household; on the other hand, however they still have secondary status within society at large, and have to face several problems arising from sexual discrimination in the labour force and violence from men. One peculiar consequence of this paradox was the construction of the myth of the »strong Caribbean matriarch«[66], which has come to represent the unique blueprint of Caribbean womanhood, obscuring in this way the complex social, economic, ethnic, and inter- and intra-group performances embraced within *matrifocal* representations. In fact, according to Christine Barrow:

»While early anthropological studies elsewhere in the Third World were clearly androcentric, obscuring women's lives and silencing their voices (Ardener 1975[67]), this was not the case in the Caribbean. The focus on family and identification of the family as the female domain meant that women, although misunderstood, were certainly not hidden and invisi-

---

[65] Barriteau, Eludine (2001): »The Political Economy of Gender in the Twentieth-Century Caribbean«, Palgrave, New York, p. 37

[66] Rowley, Michelle: »Reconceptualizing Voice, The Role of Matrifocality in Shaping, Theories and Caribbean Voices« in Mohammed, Patricia (edited by) (2002): »Gendered Realities: Essays in Caribbean Feminist Thought«, University of the West Indies Press, Barbados, p. 22

[67] Ardener, E.(1975): »Belief and the Problem of Women, in Perceiving Women«, edited by S. Ardener, Dent, London

ble in these studies. If anything, it was the men who were marginalized.«[68]

Generally speaking, the concept of matriarchy and matrifocality implies in a given society the exercise from women of a sort of power and control over their family network. More specifically the two terms are conceptually different; in fact, while matriarchy is a form of society where the power is with the women, especially the mothers of the community and their centrality it is also extended to the ideological and institutional ordering of social organization. *Matrifocality* is the kinship structure of a social system where the mother assumes structural prominence. R.T.Smith, who first coined the word, asserted that:

»The household group tend to be matrifocal in the sense that a woman in the status of »mother« is usually de facto leader of the group, and conversely the husband-father, although de jure head of the household group (if present), is usually marginal to the complex of internal relationships of the group. By »marginal« we mean that he associates relatively infrequently with other member of the group, and is on the effective ties that bind the group together.«[69]

Consequently, in the Caribbean the complexity of the family organizations and of the household is characterized by a *matrifocality* structure, rather than a matriarchy one. By analysing the various studies done on the Caribbean family structure, Patricia Mohamed asserts that:

»The interpretation of family life in the Caribbean was therefore based on several popular notions. First, the notion that the majority of families were female-centred or female headed; second, the idea that if these were female centred then males were marginal to the family; third that both of these were related to the low economic position of the males; and fourth that these were a carry over of practices from slavery.«[70]

---

68 Barrow, Christine: »Men, Women and Family in the Caribbean«, in Mohammed/Shepherd: op. cit, p. 149
69 Smith, T., Raymond (1998): »The Matrifocal Family, Power, Pluralism, and Politics«, Routledge, New York and London, p. 14
70 Mohammed, Patricia: »The Caribbean Family Revisited«, in Mohammed/Shepherd: op. cit , p. 168

Although within the Caribbean contest of multiple diversity there is an ideological unity of patriarchy, that is of female subordination and dependence, thus the patriarchal power is mediated by issues of race, class, sexual orientation, religion and other cultural considerations.

There is also another ambivalent and contradictory aspect concerning Caribbean contemporary patriarchy that has to be taken into account, that is, the so called patriarchy *in absentia*. The principal reason of this phenomenon was founded in the migration of men seeking wage employment during of the 20th century. At the beginning of the 1990s, this situation was aggravated by a massive out-migration of Caribbean population when the industrialized economies of the U.S, Great Britain and Canada endured a number of crises with severe repercussions on Caribbean counties. Indeed, according to Janet Momsen:

»Among major Caribbean social groups the paradox of patriarchal family values within a matrifocal and matrilocal society is most strongly developed within the lower-class Afro-Caribbean group, and least marked in East Indian communities. A further paradox is that the contemporary patriarchy of Caribbean societies is often patriarchy in absentia, arising from gender specific patterns of social behaviour and high levels of independent migration by men and women.«[71]

Although this explanation is partially true, it is not completely satisfying, for the simply reason that:

»Clearly no single demographic explanation can describe the system of mating and cohabitation in a community or society. Family systems are based on a complex sociology of mating rather than on simple shifts in the adult sex ratio.«[72]

The peculiarity of the Caribbean family structure, with its ambivalence and paradoxes, might not be linked just to generalized and simplified analysis. In fact, according to C. Barrow, it

---

71 Momsen, Janet: »The Double Paradox, Shaping, Theories and Caribbean Voices«, in Mohammed: op. cit, p. 51
72 Mohammed, Patricia: »Caribbean Family Revisited«, in Mohammed/Shepherd: op. cit , p. 169

might be preferable to a syncretic analysis, which takes into account the multiple factors which characterizes the complex and plural society of the Caribbean.

»The meaning of modern family practices has a long and specifically Caribbean history, dating back to the slave and indentured periods and beyond- to the cultural heritage of Africa, Europe, India and elsewhere. A Caribbean ideology of family and culture was established long ago and has persisted with remarkable tenacity over the generations. The fundamental principle of the Afro-Caribbean family system includes matrifocaly and extensive, enduring kinship networks. The closeness of the mother- child bond contrasts with relatively loose and segregated conjugal relationships.
Men are described as sexually 'irresponsible' and are more peripheral to family relationships. Well established also is the principal of marriage and legitimate children between higher status in contrast to concubinage and 'outside' children between higher status men and lower status women. Caribbean visiting and common low unions and high percentages of children born out of wedlock (varying between 60 and 70 percent in Afro-Caribbean populations) have persisted against the predictions that Caribbean peoples would adopt the nuclear family ideal with modernization and progress.«[73]

The contemporary Caribbean, less a melting pot than a mélange, remains a complex fascinating fusion of race, ethnicity, class, and culture, and the inescapable legacies of slavery and the plantation system have enormously complicated the social stratification and the gender relations within the Caribbean reality. Eudine Barriteau, in her analysis of the operations of gender system, focused principally on economical and political features of the twentieth century Caribbean, firstly clearly defining a gender system as:

»comprising a network of power relations with two principal dimensions: one ideological and the other material. [...] The material dimension reveals access to and the allocation of power, status and resources within a given community or a society. The material dimension exposes

---

[73] Barrow, Christine: »Men, Women and Family in the Caribbean Family Revisited«, in Mohammed/ Shepherd: op. cit., p. 156

how women and men gain access to or are allocated, the material and non material resources within a state or a society. [...]
The ideological dimension involves the construct of masculinity and femininity. It indicates how a given society's notion of masculinity and femininity are constructed and maintained. The ways in which masculinity and femininity are constructed reveal the gender ideologies operating in the state and society. The statements of public officials, the bureaucratic and social practices of institutions and individuals, and representations in popular culture provide evidence in what is expected of, or appropriate for, the socially constituted beings, 'women' and 'men'.«[74]

And then she tries to »locate« this imbalance of power, by questioning:

»if rapidly increasing numbers of women are being empowered by an academic environment which systematically disadvantages boys, why are women unable to translate their educational advantage into greater labour force participation and, especially, more competitive levels of remuneration? What is the wedge between women's skills level and their earning capacity? I suggest the answer lies in the differences between changes in the ideological and material relations of gender.«[75]

Given the reasons and the mechanisms that regulate the asymmetric relations of power actuated in different spheres (material and ideological) and the dynamic and interactive nature of socio/cultural and economic/political processes on a regional (Caribbean) and global (worldwide) scale, gender discourses become central to the constitution of subjectivities through the production of powerful symbols, the meanings and significance of which have widespread ramifications.

Gendered discourses are deployed both by powerful collective actors and entities and by those in resistance or opposition to them, in order to instigate or to address social change. The act of bringing to the light, better known as the act of »voicing«, challenges dichotomous representations, and, by doing so, it stresses the fact that women's realities are not locked within so-

---

74 Barriteau (2001): op. cit., p. 30
75 Ibid, p. 46

cial, ethnic, classist and ideological representations, but, on the contrary they are fluid and sensible to a constant change. On this regard Eudine Barriteau prompts that:

»These boundaries are complex and interact often in unexpected ways. They encode differing penalties, rewards and outcomes for women and men who transgress them. At times, these boundaries are rigid and overt and the penalties to women for attempting to subvert them are great. Subverting societal boundaries that encode gender relations of power invoke the greatest penalties for women in patriarchal societies. At other times the boundaries for the expression of appropriate gender identities are more nuanced. At times, societies may permit women to take on responsibilities essentially constructed as masculine as long as these do not produce a corresponding shift in gendered relations of power.
The gender contestations in the Caribbean at the start of the twenty-first century are between an inherited, socially maintained gender identity for women and the personal subjectivities, experiences, wants and needs women bring to this identity. Caribbean women are no longer content to be told who they are or should be. [...] The mechanisms for resistance have now changed. Women can now more easily reject ideas of womanhood viewed as alien to their needs and interests. It is irrelevant whether it is the majority of women or a feminist minority doing this resistance, because rejection of the phrase 'the proper role for women in society is ...' destabilizes the belief that women need the permission of others to exist.«[76]

Indeed, the transformations of cultural and political boundaries have given rise to opportunities for multiple sources of mobilising identities, as reported by Baritteau:

»The phenomenon of post- independent state actively introducing measures that generate benefits for women provokes contradictory and paradoxical outcomes. The state intervenes to free women for expanded gender-defined roles in a modernizing political economy. In the process, women gain by becoming empowered in ways that enable them to further challenge oppressive gender ideologies and identities. Compounding these developments is the fact that the strategies the state employs

---

76 Ibid, pp. 30-31

destabilizes unequal gender relations through material means. One of the consequences is that women have further mechanisms to conquest unequal ideological relations inscribed in the hierarchical gender identities and roles.«[77]

The process of transformation in which the continuous negotiation between the local and the global takes place, and the shifting identities and realities which emerge, creates identity spaces by which the material and ideological dimension are deconstructed, and from which culturally specific institutional/ representational forms are produced. The ideological dimension, like its counterpart, is fluid, dynamic, and constantly negotiated and re-negotiated through changes taking place in society at various levels.

Culture describes one way of viewing gender identity, and also the strategic process by which gender identity is represented. The importance of cultural representation is referred to the process by which meanings are produced, and the ways in which images and texts reconstruct an ideological reality, rather than reflect the original sources that they represent. Consequently, in the case of women struggles, the act of voicing through culture and cultural representations and the ambivalence of their realities become a distinctly political and agentive process.

The various forms of culture have played and still play a significant role in subverting and informing a sense of gender roles and gender identities, particularly through the display of sexual and gendered images. For instance, the act of writing is one of the most powerful roles for the emergence of women, whether consciously or subconsciously. Woman writers, in fact, share specific gender concerns in terms of how social, political and ideological factors appear from a female point of view-challenging change.

Twentieth-century women writers from the English-speaking Caribbean -for instance: Phyllis Shand Allfrey (Dominica), Zee Edgell (Belize), Merle Hodge (Trinidad), Jamaica Kincaid (Antigua), Paule Marshall (Barbados), Jean Rhys (Dominica), and Sylvia Wynter (Jamaica)- despite significant differ-

---

[77] Ibid, p.39

ences, have in common the imbalance of power between men and women in their societies and the problems of identity and inequality in relation to male dominance, inscribing fragmentations of both European and African cultures. Cultural production, indeed, is the medium through which intimacy, the unvoiced marginalization and violence, the »natural« exclusion of women from the public become a political act, whose aim is to feminize the public male domain.

On one hand the transgression of these boundaries is associated with the breakdown of social order, and the risk of chaos- and that is the case of Carnival, which actually materialize this process (both women and men participating at the public/national event and performing equally on the street), and for this reason strongly criticized by the conservative church-; on the other hand this evolution would entail a challenge to the boundaries between public and private and with it a reinvention of the domestic and the recognition of the gendered nature of economic, political and cultural phenomena.

IV. BETWEEN RITE AND PERFORMANCE

Religion and Society: From Rite to Performance and Social Change

From across the continent that someone described as dark
Ah feel a vibration, feel a riddem, feel a spark
When my spirit is feeling low, this natural mystic lift me so
Like a Congo or orisha drum
Deep in the Congo
Calling me Sandra, call
Ancient riddem
Make me feel to dance, dance, dance
Put me in a trance
Ancient riddem
I can't control me feet
I was caught by their whip
I was tied on their ship
I was used
I was wronged
That can't keep me down
Though me face get me torn
Their thong me with thorns
And the root and the rocks
Resolute like me [*]
Ancient Riddem
You hear ah rob me pain, pain, pain
Make me whole again
Ancient Ridden
Though I travel far
I, I, I
I am Africa
Ancient riddem
Brought here to this land
Which I now call me home
Trinbagonian
Though my spirit is still roam
In the ghetto born and raised
From my ancestors are taking me praise

> Through religion peace I found
> Meditation when I lay on the holy ground
> [...]
> Now I am free as a bird,
> Liberty is the word
> West Indian, Caribbean,
> African, Yoruba Queen
> My skin that may burn
> With crosses they burn
> No, I wouldn't be denied
> There is peace in this time
> [...]
> Ancient Riddem
> Deep within me soul
> Red green black and gold
> [...]
> Ancient riddem
> Be my destiny
> Come come come
> Set me truly free.
> [...]*
> (Singing Sandra, Ancient Riddem)

Rituals of various kinds are a feature of almost all known human societies, past or present. It generally refers to any customary observance or practice, that is, human experience and perception in forms which are enriched by imagination, making reality more complex and unnatural. Ritual is the mundane instrument that spheres of human experience assume. In these terms, ritual is part of distinct situations where routine acts, with their contextually determined meanings are exaggerated, stylised, refined, and set into a pattern of expressive sequences of visual and auditory symbols.

Although »ethologically speaking, ritual is ordinary behaviour transformed by means of condensation, exaggeration, repetition, and rhythm into specialized sequences of behaviour serving specific functions usually having to do with mating, hierarchy, or territoriality«[78], it is never simply or solely a matter of routine, or habit. It is, in fact, a unique structure whose ele-

---

*   My transcription: it may contain mistakes
78 Schechner (1993): op.cit., p. 228

ments do not belong to it alone; none of its elements is unique to ritual, but their mutual interaction and how they relate to it.

Throughout the last decades, ritual's multicoded redundancies have been analysed and contextualised by different currents of thoughts, which gave rise to several important styles of interpretation- evolutionary, sociological, and psychological- from which new fields of scholarship emerged. Ritual, in fact, has been considered:

»1) as a part of the evolutionary development of animals
2) as structures with formal qualities and definable relationships
3) as symbolic system of meanings
4) as performative actions or process
5) as experience«[79]

The schema above implies that:

»These categories overlap. It is also clear that rituals are not safe deposit vaults of accepted ideas, but in many cases dynamic performative systems generating new materials and recombining traditional actions in new ways.«[80]

Ritual, therefore, might be understood as an authoritative mode of symbolic discourse and a powerful instrument for the evocation of those sentiments (affinity and estrangement) out of which society is constructed. The relationship between the ordinary and the non-ordinary in terms of social action is the result of a processing set of actions, performed mainly for their symbolic value mostly prescribed by a religion or by a tradition of a community, which becomes a fundamental part of human culture and a peculiar aid in the process of creating a sense of group identity and social bonds.

The socio-cultural dimension of ritual denotes an historically transmitted precedents of meanings embodied in symbols, that is »a system of inherited conceptions expressed in symbolic forms by means of which men communicate, perpetuate, and

---

79 Ibid.
80 Ibid.

develop their knowledge about attitudes toward life«[81]. Indeed, according to Clifford Geertz:

»So far as culture patterns, that is, systems or complexes of symbols, are concerned, the generic trait which is of first importance for us here is that they are extrinsic sources of information. By 'extrinsic', I mean only that-unlike genes, for example- they lie outside the boundaries of the individual organism as such in that intersubjective world of common understandings into which all human individuals are born, in which they pursue their separate careers, and which they leave persisting behind them after they die. By 'sources of information', I mean only that – like genes- they provide a blueprint or template in terms of which processes external to themselves can be given a definitive form. As the order of bases in a strand of DNA forms a coded program, a set of instructions, or a recipe, for the synthesis of the structurally complex protein which shape organic functioning, so culture patterns provide such programs for the institution of the social and psychological processes which shape public behaviour. [...]
For psychological and social systems, and for cultural models that we would not ordinarily refer to as 'theories', but rather as 'doctrines', 'melodies', or 'rites', the case is in no way different. Unlike genes, and other nonsymbolic information sources, which are only models for, not models of, culture patterns have an intrinsic double aspect: they give meaning, that is objective conceptual form, to social and psychological reality both by shaping themselves to it and by shaping it to themselves.«[82]

In other words, Geertz sees religion and ritual as a consequence, as a cultural system of symbols adding significance to people's motivation and emotions by giving unified and coherent patterns to the meaning of life. A world view is lived out through rites and thereby acquires concrete meaning for the private individuals.

This analysis could be compared to Saussure's famous studies about the language structure. Saussure, in fact, pointed out that language is a system of signs all of whose parts interrelate

---

[81] Geertz, Clifford (2000): »The Interpretation of Cultures«, Basic Books, New York, p. 89
[82] Ibid, pp. 92-93

and interact organically, holding in a specific society, and therefore considered as a social phenomenon. Consequently he divided the sign in two different units: *signifiant* (something that means, or the sound image, »the psychological imprint of the sound, the impression that it makes on our senses«[83]) and *signifié*, (something that is meant, or the concept, which is more abstract than the sound image), which are constantly in mutual relation, for the fact that one element cannot exist without the other and vice versa.

For the realization of a language is necessary to a community of speakers, therefore language has a value only within a specific reality and never exists apart from the social fact. If, generally speaking, a system is a matter of convention in a specific society and at specific time, then the mutability of the language is affected as well by historical (time) and social forces in an apparently contradictory way. In fact:

»Time, which insures the continuity of language, wields another influence apparently contradictory to the first: the more or less rapid change of linguistic signs. [...] the sign is exposed to alteration because it perpetuates itself. What predominates in all changes is the persistence of the old substance; disregard for the past is only relative. That is why the principle of changes is based on principals of continuity.«[84]

Moreover:

»If we consider language in time, without a community of speakers [...] we probably would notice no change; time would not influence language. Conversely, if we considered the community of speakers without considering time, we would not see the effect of the social forces that influences language. [...]
Language is no longer free, for time will allow the social forces at work on it to carry out their effects. This brings us back to the principle of continuity, which cancels freedom. But continuity necessarily implies

---

[83] Saussure, Ferdinand de (1974): »Course in General Linguistics«, Collins, Fontana, p.66
[84] Ibid, p 74

change, varying degrees of shifts in the relationship between the signified and the signifier.«[85]

This inner duality of language and the relations of its elements should be analysed, according to Saussure, by two different and equally valid approaches: a diachronic and a synchronic analysis. That is to say that a synchronic study would deal with those that are general in a specific community, within a period in which they can be treated as unchanging; whilst a diachronic might instead examine the evolution of a language throughout the history, comparing the relations among successive elements that are not perceived by the same collective consciousness. Thus, by agreeing to the fact that myth and ritual (beside their differences) are a cultural system of symbols, Saussure's analysis might be borrowed for a better understanding of these phenomena.

According to Mircea Eliade, the epiphanic representations (through myth, religious ceremonies, and ritual performances) of the symbolic structure appear as the interactive social »*poesis*« (from greek πόιεω, which means to make) of the human reality:

»The sacred tree, the sacred stone are not adored as stone or tree; they are worshipped precisely because they are hierophanies, because they show something that is no longer stone or tree but sacred, the ganz andere. [...]
By manifesting the sacred, any object becomes something else, yet it continues to remain itself, for it continues to participate in its surrounding cosmic milieu. A sacred stone remains a stone; apparently (or, more precisely, from the profane point of view), nothing distinguishes it from all other stones. But for those to whom a stone reveals itself as a sacred, its immediate reality is transmuted into supernatural reality. In other words, for those who have religious experiences all nature is capable of revealing itself as a cosmic sacrality. The cosmos in its entirety can become a hierophany.
The man of the archaic societies tends to live as much as possible in the sacred or in close proximity to consecrated objects. The tendency is perfectly understandable, because for primitives as for the man of all pre-

---

85 Ibid, p 78

modern societies, the sacred is equivalent to a power, and in the last analysis, to reality. The sacred is saturated with being. Sacred power means reality and at the same time enduringness and efficacy. The polarity sacred-profane is often expressed as an opposition between real and unreal or pseudoreal. [...] Thus it is easy to understand that religious man deeply desires to be, to participate in reality, to be saturated with power. [...]

When the sacred manifests itself in any hierophany, there is not only a break in the homogeneity of space; there is also revelation of an absolute reality, opposed to the nonreality of the vast surrounding expanse. The manifestation of the sacred ontologically funds the world.«[86]

Indeed, similarly to verbalized language, myth and ritual are also a form of communication, in the sense that both project model of conceptual and intangible realities or human experiences in a concrete and visible structure, which, in its turn, brings about reciprocal personal contact and preserve it.

Victor Turner, one of the most famous social anthropologist of the 20th century, who dedicated his life to the study of ritual, symbols and theatre in relation to nature of society and to the social aspects of human beings, pointed out, reconsidering the semantic studies about the function of the language, that:

»Symbols, both as sensorily perceptible vehicles (significants) and as a set of 'meanings' (signifies), are essentially involved in multiple variability of the essentially living, conscious, emotional and volitional creatures who employ them not only to give order to the universe they inhabit, but creatively to make use also of disorder, both by overcoming or reducing it in particular cases and by its means questioning former axiomatic principles that have become a fetter on the understanding and manipulation of contemporary things.«[87]

Both myth and ritual satisfy the needs of a society and the relative employ (exercise) of one or the other will depend upon the particular necessitates of the individuals at a particular time

---

[86] Eliade, Mircea (1959): »The Sacred and the Profane, the Nature of Religion«, Harvest/HBJ Book, New York and London, pp. 12-21

[87] Turner, Victor (1979): »Process, Performance, and Pilgrimage«, Concept Publishing Company, New Delhi, p. 14

and in a particular society, since they are characterized by a fluctuant relationship of intricate mutual interdependence, related to a specific culture in a specific time and place.

Clyde Kluchohn describes myth as the »ideal pattern«, whereas ritual the »behavioural« (action) »pattern«, since the differences (although their common psychological and functional basis) between the two, although hardly negligible, are in large measure a matter of genre, ritual discourse being primarily gestural and dramatic; mythical discourse, verbal and narrative. The one, in fact, tends to dramatize (through a repetitive activity) in a symbolic way the fundamental needs of a society, whether economic, political, biological or sexual; whilst the other tends to rationalize (in the sense that the use of verbal narration is associated to the concept of »conventionality« and »arbitrariness« deployed by Saussure[88]) the same needs through the use of the logos. Thus, summarizing and as a consequence to what Fontenrose pointed out, that is:

»The ritual gives to the myth the very names of its characters, much of its detail, and an aetiological character. The myth acts more slowly upon ritual, which is conservative. At first it may be limited to interpretation of ritual features. Gradually it may impose features upon the ritual, so that a rudimentary ritual drama may come into being. Then men may think of including in the festival program a mimetic representation of the mythical narrative through dance, song, gesture, action; then true ritual drama is born.«[89]

Which is to say, according to Walter Burket:

»In this way, by mutually affirming each other, myth and ritual became a strong force in forming a cultural tradition, even though their origins were different.«[90]

---

88 See quotation corresponding to footnote 18
89 Fontenrose, Joseph (1974): »Python, A Study of Delphic Myth and Its Origins«, Biblo-Tannen., New York, p. 464
90 Burkert, Walter (1998): »Homo Necans, in Segal Robert A, The Myth and Ritual Theory«, Blackwell Publishers, Malden, Oxford, p. 346

In other words, this perspective of religious phenomena is one of the corollaries of Durkheim's work on the social aspects/function of religion. The famous French sociologist of the 20th century, in fact, was one of the first (if not the first) who was concerned with what religion does socially, by being firmly convinced, after studying the totemic religion among Australian aborigines, that religion binds members of society, by becoming consequentially the symbolic expression of social experience. Thus, by picturing religion as a matter of social images and behaviours, he asserts:

»[...] religion is an eminently social thing. Religious representations are collective representations that express collective realities; rites are ways of acting that are born in the midst of assembled groups and whose purpose is to evoke, maintain, or recreate certain mental states of those groups. But if the categories are of religious origin, then they must participate in what is common to all religion: They, too, must be a social thing, products of collective thought.«[91]

Furthermore, by seeing mythology (considering Durkheim's perspective of myth and rite as religious phenomena) as »the collection of beliefs common to the group. How the society imagines man and the world is expressed in the traditions whose memory the mythology perpetuates; it is a morality and a cosmology at the same time as it is a history«, and ritual as a practice which »serves and can only serve to maintain the vitality of those beliefs and to prevent their memory from being obliterated- in other words, to revitalize the most essential elements of the collective consciousness and conscience. Through this rite, the group periodically revitalizes the sense it has for itself and its unity; the nature of individual as a social being is strengthened at the same time«[92], he pointed out that religion functions to ensure the unconscious priority of communal identification.

Ritual might be considered as a transformative phenomenon for its nature of being »more fittingly applied to forms of reli-

---

91 Durkheim, Emile (c1995): »The Elementary Forms of Religious Life«, The free Press, New York, p. 9
92 Ibid., p. 35

gious behaviour associated with social transition«[93], because »the historical variation of the rule that seems to govern our present logic show that, far from being encoded from eternity in the mental constitution of man, the rule depends at least in part upon historical, hence social factors«[94].

Although the nature of ritual and its structure and components might have various analogies and similarities with language (and for this reason both phenomena have been parallely related), there is a peculiar difference in the development process. In fact, as Saussure pointed out:

»The bond between the signifier and signified is arbitrary.
The word symbol has been used to designate the linguistic sign, or more specifically, what is here called signifier. Principal I in particular weighs against the use of this term. One characteristic of the symbol is that it is never wholly arbitrary; it is not empty, for there is the rudiment of a natural bond between the signifier and the signified.
In fact every means of expression in a society is based, in principle, on collective behaviour or- what amounts to the same thing- on convention.«[95]

Van Gennep, in his well known work »Les Rites de Passage«, adduces this lack of a complete arbitrariness to the cycles of nature and human life, which are characterized by a ritualized transition through a social order.

»Thus we encounter a wide degree of general similarity among ceremonies of birth, childhood, social puberty, betrothal, marriage, pregnancy, fatherhood, initiation into religious society, and funerals. In this respect, man's life resembles nature, from which neither the individual nor the society stands independent. The universe itself is governed by a periodicity which has repercussion on human life, with stages and transitions, movements forward, and periods of relative inactivity.«[96]

---

93 Turner Victor (1967): »The Forest of Symbols: Aspects of Ndembu Ritual«, Cornell University Press, Ithaca (NY), London, p. 95
94 Ibid, p. 12
95 Ibid, p. 67-68
96 Van Gennep, Arnold (1960): »The Rites of Passage«, Routledge and Kegan Paul, London, p. 4

Indeed, in order to try to dominate the imperative of biological changes, ritual practices become a necessity, which accompany crisis, that is, the passage of one status to another. Furthermore he asserts that:

»Because of the importance of these transitions, I think it legitimate to single out rites of passage as a special category, which under further analysis may be subdivided into rites of separation, transition rites, and rites of incorporation.«[97]

Through these sequences of activities, in fact, rituals affect the social/individual removal from one status to other, by dramatizing the change, creating a liminal status, where the prior conditions are suspended for a circumscribed period of time, and finally incorporating the individuals/group in the new social/natural dimension.

His study on the internal organisation of ritual and how it affects/orchestrates the dynamics of social and individual (always related within the society) changes open new perspectives on the relationship of ritual to social organization. In fact, his theories concerning the structure of ritual were developed into an innovative analytical model by Victor Turner, as he asserts:

»I wish to consider some of the sociocultural proprieties of the »liminal period« in that class of rituals which Arnold Van Gennep has definitively characterized as 'rites de passage'. If our basic model of society is that of a »structure of positions«, we must regard the period of margin or 'liminality' as an interstructural situation«[98]

The main impact of Victor Turner's thesis was on the study of the mechanism of rituals and roles that play in the ordering and re-ordering of social relations and changes. From his point of view ritual practice- given its capacity of generating ideas and social arrangements that challenge the existing stability- on one hand affirms the social order, whilst, on the other hand, facilitates disordered inversions of that order: through such a process, the original order is simultaneously legitimated and modi-

---

97 Ibid, p. 12
98 Turner (1967): op. cit., p. 93

fied most of the times by an inversion of the existing models - either in its basic structure or by moving people from one status to another.

Although Turner, in the wake of Van Gennep's analysis, describes ritual as the element which mediates the transition of a community from the structure to the anti/structure, to a successive new structure, the emphasis now is upon what flows and changes; innovation, not duration, becomes the keynote. In other words, Turner sees ritual as an ideal or symbolic layer of a real social process and liminality, as a restricted period of social limbo and as an anti/structural moment of reversal which is the creative source not only for ritual, but for culture in general. Turner, in fact, asserts that:

»as I have written elsewhere, ritual is not necessarily a bastion of social conservatism; its symbols do not merely condense cherished sociocultural values. Rather, through its liminal process, it holds the generating source of culture and structure.«[99]

Indeed, Turner recasts this process into a more fundamental dialectic between the social order (structure) and a period of social disorder which generates a temporal anti/structure, that Turner termed *communitas*.

»It is as though there are here two major 'models' for human interrelatedness, juxtaposed and alternating. The first is of society structured and differentiated, and often hierarchical system of politico-legal economic positions with many types of evaluations, separating men in terms of 'more' or 'less'. The second, which emerges recognizably in the liminal period, is of a society as unstructured or rudimentarily structured and relatively undifferentiated comitatus, community, or even communion of equal individuals who submit together to the general authority of the ritual elders.«[100]

---

99 Turner, Victor (1986): »The Anthropology of Performance«, PAJ Publications, New York, p. 158
100 Turner, Victor (1969): »The Ritual Process, Structure and Anti/Structure«, Routledge & Kegan Paul, London, p. 96

According to Turner, society is always a dynamic process, consisting of two mutually interdependent and interactive poles that he came to call »structure« and »communitas«, which is regulated by a constant dialectical relation. Here, he echoes Max Gluckman's theory on ritualization of social conflicts, by stressing the aspect of ritual as a social action, which has the vital function of constantly re-creating, not just reaffirming, social unity.

Max Gluckman in his analysis of the so called »ritual of rebellion«, pointed out that:

»The acceptance of the established order as right and good, and even sacred, seems to allow unbridled license, very rituals of rebellion, for the order itself keeps this rebellion within bounds. Hence to act the conflicts, whether directly or by inversion or in other symbolical forms, emphasizes the social cohesion within which the conflicts exist. As the social order always contains a division of rights and duties, and of privileges and powers as against responsibilities, the ritual enactment of the order states its rightness.«[101]

In Gluckman's functionalist approach, the role of rituals is to sustain a society's equilibrium and secure solidarity among its members. In his perspective, rituals are seen as mechanisms which ensure societal unity that may be achieved in spite of social conflicts and competing social norms and values.

Although Gluckman diverged from the classic functionalist view, he still stresses the conservative results of ritual, while Turner sees it as socially transformative. In his analysis of ritual function within society, he extends the concept of liminality to include post-industrial, non ritual phenomena, by coining the term »liminoid« to apply to functional equivalent, making a distinction between the liminal phenomena, which are characteristic of the pre-industrial society, and liminoid, which is the playlike feature of the postindustrial society. Turner explains that:

---

101 Gluckman, Max (1955): »Custom and Conflict in Africa«, Blackwell, Oxford, Basil, p. 125

»(1)Liminal phenomena tend to predominate in tribal and early agrarian societies possesing what Durkheim has called 'mechanical solidarity', and dominated by what Henry Maine has called »status«. Liminoid phenomena flourish in society with 'organic solidarity', bonded reciprocally by 'contractual' relations, and generated by and following the industrial revolution, though they perhaps begin to appear on the scene in city-states on their way to becoming empires [...]. But they first begin clearly to develop in Western Europe in nascent capitalistic societies, with the beginning of industrialization and mechanization, the transformation of labour into a commodity, and the appearance of the real social classes.

(2)Liminal phenomena tend to be collective, concerned with calendrical, biological, social-structural rhythms or with crisis in social processes whether these result from internal adjustments or external adaptations or remedial measures. Thus they appear at what may be called 'natural breaks', natural disjunctions in the flow of natural and social processes. They are thus enforced by sociocultural 'necessity', but they contain in nuce 'freedom' and the potentiality for the formation of new ideas, symbols, models, beliefs. Liminoid phenomena may be collective (and when they are so, are often directly derived from liminal antecedents) but are more characteristically individual products though they often have collective, or 'mass' effects. They are not cyclical, but continuously generated, though in the time and places apart from work setting assigned to 'leisure' activities

(3)Liminal phenomena are centrally integrated into the total social process, forming with all its other aspects a complete whole. [...] Liminoid phenomena develop apart from the central economic and political processes, along the margins, in the interfaces and interstices of central and servicing institutions- they are plural, fragmentary and experimental in character.

(4) Liminal phenomena [...] They differ from the preliminal or postliminal collective representation in that they are often reversals, inversion, disguises, negations, antithesis of quotidian, 'positive' or 'profane' collective representations. But they share their mass collective character. Liminoid phenomena tend to be more idiosyncratic, quirky, to be generated by specific names, individuals and in particular groups- 'schools' circles, and coteries- they have to compete for one another for general recognition and are thought of at first as ludic offerings placed for sale on the 'free' market- this is at least true of liminoid phenomena in nascent capitalistic and democratic-liberal societies. [...]

(5) Liminal phenomena (my italics) tend to be ultimately eufunctional even when seemingly 'inversive' for the working of the social structure [...] Liminoid phenomena (my italics), on the other hand, are often parts of social critiques or even revolutionary manifestos-books, plays, paintings, etc., exposing the injustices, inefficiencies, and immoralities of the mainstream economic and political structures and organization.«[102]

Indeed ritual is worklike (*ergic*) in liminal pre-industrial settings, and playlike (*anergic*) in liminoid, post-industrial ones, since, according to Turner, »[...] for most people liminoid is felt to be freer than the limina, a matter of choice, not obligation [...]. One works at the liminal, one plays with the liminoid.«[103] In other words, in the liminal events in pre-industrial society there are no sharp distinctions between work and play, since work is a function of the liminal ritual experience, and play is also a function within a given ritual. Religious obligation characterizes the liminal ('liturgy is derived from the Greek '*leos*' or '*laos*', 'the people', and '*ergon*' 'work')[104], while »optation« characterizes the liminoid.

Liminoid phenomena, existing as a product of the work/leisure polarization of industrial and post-industrial social order, mainly differ from the liminal because of their nature of »independent and critical source [...] independent domain of creative activity«- which is potentially experimental and innovative- and »antistructure« which »can generate and store a plurality of alternative models for living«[105], whilst, by contrast, the same term »antistructure« applied to the liminal phase of pre-industrial society, is pictured as »functional, in the sense of being a special duty or performance required in the course of work or activity; its very reversals and inversions tend to compensate for rigidities or unfairnesses of normative«[106] Consequentially, ritual experience, universally speaking, provides human-beings a means of self-reflexivity, a space in which past and future merge and interlace in a flowing present activity.

---

102 Turner, Victor (1982:) »From Ritual to Theatre, The Human Seriousness of Play«, PAJ Publication, New York, pp. 53-55.
103 Ibid.
104 Ibid, p. 30
105 Ibid, p. 33
106 Ibid, p. 52

At both the micro and macro levels, both the lives of individuals, their mutual relationships, and the more public and collective processes –from social movements to wars, revolutions and political transitions-continue to depend on symbolic communications and cultural interactions that find their expression in ritualised processes or, in complex societies, in ritual-like activities.

According to Turner, who echoes Dilthey's notion of *Erlebnis*, experience is never complete until it has been expressed, until it has found expression through human symbolic action. Experience becomes objectified, universal and abstract, through expression. In fact he asserts:

»every type of cultural performance, including ritual, ceremony, carnival theatre, and poetry, is explanation and explication of life itself, as Dilthey often argued. Through the performance process itself, what is normally sealed up, inaccessible to everyday observation and reasoning, in depth of the sociocultural life, is drawn forth. [...]'Meaning' is squeezed out of an event which has either been directly experienced by the dramatist or poet, or cries out penetrative, imaginative understanding (Verstehen). An experience is itself a process which presses out to an expression which completes it. Here the etymology of 'performance'. [...]
from the Old French parfournir, to 'complete' or 'carry out throughly'. A performance, then, is the proper finale of an experience.«[107]

Play and ritual are symbolic expressions of life experience that represent, even exaggerate, the lived social drama of individuals and communities, as Turner himself pointed out:

»I came to see performances of ritual as distinct phases in the social processes whereby groups became adjusted to internal changes (whether brought about by personal or factional dissensions and conflicts of norms or by technical or organizational innovations), and adapted to their external environment (social and cultural, as well as physical and biotic).«[108]

---

107 Ibid, p. 13
108 Ibid, pp. 21-22

Indeed, ritual is the ideal, symbolic dramatized expression of a real social process that represents the life experiences, the social dramas of individuals and communitas.

Turner introduced the notion of social drama in his work »Schism and Continuity« regarding Ndembu social organization, as a device to look beneath the surface of social regularities into the hidden contradictions and eruptions of conflict in the social structure. He described four main phases of the social drama cycle: (1) a breach of regular norm-governed social relationships between persons or groups of a social unit; (2) a crisis or extension of the breach, unless the conflict can be sealed off quickly; (3) adjustive and redressive mechanisms brought into operation by leading members of the social group; and (4) reintegration of the disturbed social group or social recognition of an irreparable breach or schism (Turner 1957: 91-94). He then extrapolated this concept of social drama from the specific, in order to apply it as a universal processual form which »represents a perpetual challenge to all aspirations to perfections in social and political organization«.[109]

According to Turner social drama might be considered as a narration of life experience, and experience is never complete until it has been represented, that is, until it has found expression through human symbolic action. So, from his perspective, the term »drama« describes some basic shapes of human behaviour.

The subjunctive mood, indeed, the expression of the potentiality implicit in the redressive phase, finds its completion in performances, which are, according to Richard Schechner- the performance theorist who utilized Turner's concept as a maker of aesthetic performances- »make-believe, in play, for fun«[110]. As Schechner pointed out, »also not only narratives but the bodily actions of drama express crisis, schism, and conflicts«[111], and consequentially: »performance is an illusion of an illusion, and as such, might be considered more 'truthful', more 'real'

---

[109] Turner, Victor: (1957): »Schism and Continuity in an African Society, A Study of Ndembu Village Life«, Manchester University Press, Manchester, p. 71

[110] Schechner, Richard (2003): »Performance Theory«, Routledge, New York and London, p. xix

[111] Ibid, p. xviii

than ordinary experience. This too was Aristotle's opinion in his poetics where theatre did not so much reflect living as essentialize it, present paradigms of it.«[112]

The primary function of ritual is to produce a »social body« endowed with new schemes designed to operate in the social world. In other words, ritual practice generate alternative symbolic systems which are dialectically opposed and, in specific periods of time, alternated to the normative symbolic systems that provide cultural metaphor for roles, status and behaviour.

The cultural/normative discourses, practice and institutions that reflect the consistent inequality within the society, are supported by ideologies aimed to justify the unequal distributions of power by naturalizing it.

Gender differences are ideologically constructed, in a way that the sexual and biological diversity is aligned with certain inequalities, which, in their turn, bring to the ideological transformation of biologically female into the socially feminine. The social interaction which produces gender partially takes place through cultural and religious phenomena. That is to say, that the conveyance of concepts and values expressed through oral, visual and ritual means, through the responses to, or the manipulations of those messages, becomes a system of symbol, which is extremely gendered, for it is where the perpetuations or re-creations of gender concept, symbolic meanings, social/structural divisions and individual gendered identity take place.

The *par excellence* dimension of the construction of public and symbolic feminine is women's participation or absence in religious and ritual practices. In every religious/symbolic system the presence of women and their representation is strikingly related with their sexual and reproductive status, while in the same contest the male sexual status is most of the time irrelevant, in the sense that it does not determine their participation in ritual. Female metaphors and symbols are mainly reduced to their sexual function, and consequentially they have always had one-dimensional characters in mythology and ritual action. This generates a further contradiction, that is, the construction of a dualist image of women in the collective memory.

---

112 Ibid, p. xix

The general separation of the sexes can be seen as part of a larger system of dichotomies and oppositions, in which ritual practice, although invented sometimes for the sake of entertainment, they mainly reflect a living and burning reality that exists in the psyche and culture of a people. Every voluntary or involuntary mental construct in a myth, legend, phantasm, dream, visitation, hallucination, or apparition may be said to be real, or to be at least a fragment of something that occurred either consciously or unconsciously. Religious phenomena are thus a vital ingredient of human civilization and as such, they are experienced and/or understood according to cultural canon of the members of a given society: they answered a need, an inner pulsing, an aspiration, a necessity for a defensive mechanism, or a yearning, on both a personal and collective level.

From this perspective ritual practice answers a specific need in both the individual and the society. It plays a subtle role in the formulation of an ethos—aggressive, devouring, anguishing, loving, or otherwise. Ritual may lend continuity to life and may bring order to disorder, making comprehensible that which goes beyond individual understanding and control. The popularity of certain rituals or myths at particular junctures in civilization explains the needs and deficiencies as well as the positive attributes of a given society, since the subtleties of society and culture may be better acknowledged and explained via the ambiguities, discrepancies, contradictions, and paradoxes expressed and exaggerated through ritual. Attitudes toward humanity –women, in particular– toward nature, learning, logic, and love are symbolically projected in mythical narratives or in ritual performances.

The recognition of a role and a considerable position in the religious sphere emerging from the social collective unconscious might be, therefore, of crucial importance for all, and especially for women, who have been victimized for so many centuries by man's projections. In fact, throughout history, women have always been pictured as Archetypal mothers, wives, daughters, and sisters, as humans and/or goddesses, abound in myths in all of their intricacies, enigmas, and labyrinthine behavioural patterns as they live out their credos; they have been adored, idolized, or iconicized, and thus dehumanized, and transformed into cult objects.

How gender social system affects performance contexts and vice versa is complex, as is the nature and extent of women's genres in specific cultures. Women participation in religious, folkloristic sphere might be expressive of women's attitudes, values, anxieties, and worldview, in such a way that it can be of considerable importance in interpreting society and women's role within it, since in a number of cultures they have always played a fundamental position as song makers and singers, shamans and cerimonialists, often possessing uniquely female folklore, being the savers and conservators of beliefs, rites, superstitions, rituals, and customs.

In those societies where relations of dominance and submission are characterized above all in sexual terms, the gendered nature of ritual practice is always implicit; in many cultures, in fact, as pointed out by Judith Hoch-Smith, »female sexuality is seen as a disruptive, chaotic force that must be controlled or co-opted by men, periodically purified, and at times destroyed.«[113] Indeed, despite ritual which is socially- therefore ideologically-constructed on a system of symbols confirms the traditional and restricted notion of female's identity, »the ritual sphere thus emerges as an arena of constant renegotiation between women and ideologies that governed their lives, an arena on which women act out ritual scenarios alternating between cooperation with that governance and resistance to it.«[114]

Cross cultural, historical and formal similarities can be found in analysing female religious participation, beliefs, female metaphors and performances, since the marginalized and inferior position of women within a patriarchal society allows them to become critics of the normative structure from a *communitas* perspective, which in its turn creates the sentiment of wholeness and posits the model of an undifferentiated whole whose units are total human beings.

The roles concerning the religious and traditional sphere played in ritual by women in the Caribbean, might be the ap-

---

113 Hoch-Smith, Juidith (edited by) (c1978): »Women in Ritual and Symbolic Rules«, Plenum, New York, p. 3
114 Goff, Barbara (2004): »Citizen Bacchae, Women's Ritual Practice in Ancient Greece«, University of California Press, Berkley, p. 4

propriate example of how ritual practices could be influenced, hybridized and reshaped on inherited models of agency (Western and African traditions), whose evolution acquires both universal-diachronical- and peculiar– synchronical- meanings. That is to say that Caribbean society, due to its particular history, has been and still is the protagonist of a continuous process of hybridization, which, because of its nature, is the source of phenomena that from different perspectives are simultaneously cross cultural and typical Caribbean.

Today, there are significant survivals of the Yoruba culture in North and South America and the Caribbean. This influence is mostly pronounced in religion and in other syncretic cultural expressions and production like carnival (music and masquerade), theatre and literature (the use of a Creole language). Moreover, in the process of cultural hybridization, Yoruba religion and its ancestral traditions have influenced the birth of new religions such as *Candomble* and *Macumba* in Brazil; *Sàngó* in Trinidad and Tobago, Grenada, and Barbados; *Kele* in St Lucia; and *Santeria* in Cuba, Venezuela and United States. Yoruba influence is also evident in the *voodoo* (vodou) in Haiti and New Orleans. The Yoruba comprise several clans– the majority of the Yoruba live in southwestern Nigeria, there are also substantial indigenous Yoruba communities in Benin, Ghana and Togo – which are bound together by language, traditions, and religious beliefs and practices.

The keynote of their lives is their religion, which forms the foundation and the all-governing principle of life for them. As far as they are concerned, the full responsibility of all the affairs of life belongs to the Deity; through all the circumstances of life, through all its changing scenes, its joys and troubles, it is the Deity who is in control. The religion of the Yoruba permeates their lives so much that it expresses itself in multifarious ways. It forms the theme of songs, makes topics for minstrelsy, finds vehicles in myths, folktales, proverbs and sayings, and is the basis of philosophy and art. In fact, according to Babatunde Lawal:

»Broadly speaking, the Yoruba, like other African peoples, use art to reinforce life and to ensure social and cosmic harmony. At the religious level, art is used to honor and communicate with divinities (o'ris'a),

whose spiritual support is deemed vital to individual and corporate survival. [...]
Several religious festivals take place in a given community every year to promote the spiritual well being of people, providing a forum for celebrating and reaffirming their unity. One of the most popular of these festivals is the Egungun. This features colorful masked figures representing the spirits of deceased ancestors who are visiting the earth to renew acquaintance with their living descendants.«[115]

These beliefs and practice have also important implications for understanding the power gender relationships in Yoruba society. As Margaret Thompson Drewal pointed out:

»the formalization of sex roles lends itself easily to deconstruction, not only by ethnographers, but by the performers themselves. In this way performers use the structure of ritual to reflect on gender and sex role divisions. [...]
The rules, such as they are, relate directly to Yoruba concepts of power in the construction of gender.«[116]

In Yoruba art, for instance, women are pictured as mother, priestess, bird, and man's partner, since their concepts of female and male power mainly derive from shared cultural values in the interpretation of biological factors, expressed as binary opposites. As in many African societies, the idealized role of mother, house and family caring wife, clashes with the daily reality of women carrying on their own activity and being economically independent, as for example Yoruba women have been able traditionally to obtain a great deal of economic independence from their husbands through their marketing activities. In male/dominated societies where females gain authority, the male counterpart's resentment is focused on venerating the biological roles of women and, simultaneously, on the contrary they picture them as witches, or sometimes prostitutes repre-

---

115 Lawal, Bambatund (1996): »The Gélédè Spectacle«, University of Washington Press, Seattle and London, pp. 15-16.
116 Drewal, Thompson, Margaret (1992): »Yoruba Ritual, Performers, Play, Agency«, Indiana University Press, Bloomington, Indianapolis, p. 173

senting the sexual power hold by women over men. On this regard Drewall explains:

>>According to Yoruba belief, the concentration of vital force in women, their ase, their power to bring things into existence, to make things happen, creates extraordinary potential, that can manifest itself in both positive and negative ways. Phrases such as 'one with two faces' (oloju meji), 'one with two bodies (abara meji), and one of two colors (alawo meji) aptly express this duality and allude to their alleged powers of transformations. The Yoruba word for this special power is aje, which has been translated in the literature with 'witchcraft' or witch. [...]
Unlike the predominantly negative connotation of the English word 'witch', elderly women are not necessarily either antisocial or the personification of evil. Rather they form an important segment of the population in any town and are given respect, affection and deference. Because of their special powers they are thought to have greater access to Yoruba deities.<<[117]

Generally speaking, in the African religious sphere the role played by one sex is to be seen as complementing that played by the other, and the male-female relationship is the ground of this complementarily, and considering the significant roles played by women, it could be possible to speak about indispensability of the women's presence in ritual, since certain ritual and ceremonies cannot be carried out without the presence or participation of women, and in cases where they are performed with the physical women's absence, the female attendance is symbolically reproduced. In fact, although even to this day, the African world is still to a greater or lesser extent a man's world in the sense that woman's position in the society is still largely subservient, it is the nature of the religious stage on which African women find themselves, where the ambiguities of gender and power become explicit.

Parallely, in the ancient Greek society, evidence of women's activity can be found more frequently in the religious field, since ritual practice afforded them a public presence and voice. Ancient Greek culture and society, which are considered in the western imaginary »the cradle of the European civilization«,

---

[117] Ibid, pp. 177-178

were in reality a male dominated society, based on a misogynic ideology and structured on a patriarchal societal organization, where the segregation of women within the domestic domain was the norm.

Although women were invisible as individual citizen, women's ritual life provided the source for their importance in the community; it publicly sanctioned and validated women's role in the community. Since religion played a central role in the lives of the ancient Greeks, and therefore calendars were filled with festivals, women had frequent opportunities to move freely and independently within their communities, thereby providing a balance to the restrictions placed on women's roles in other areas of society.

According to Barbara Goff, »ritual discourse aims at producing women who function well within a male dominated culture by successfully internalizing a version of themselves useful to that culture«[118], but, »although the ancient city, or polis, may be defined by its exclusion of women, children, and slaves, who cannot be citizens, the ritual sphere provides for women, at least, a parapolitical form of activity and identity, that partly remedies their exclusion«[119].

In other words, although the women's participation in ritual practices is related to their biological nature, that is with fertility, (connected with the agricultural year) and they were also considered especially permeable to the influence of the non-human (as possessed devotees of Dionysus or as the chosen prophetesses of Apollo), and therefore determined by the models of female identity characteristic of Greek culture, the religious sphere might be considered a possible (subjunctive) and privileged area of dissent. Religious, ritual and cultural practices, indeed, could be arenas where women's behaviour and activities unsettle conventional categorizations, and from which leadership and assertiveness spill over into other arenas. In fact, according to Barbara Goff:

»ritual activity, far from being a temporary diversion from daily life, constituted a constant element constituted of the texture of lived experi-

---

118 Goff : op. cit., p.5
119 Ibid, p.6

ence, and that it regularly required women to exercise significant presence and agency in the public realm. Ritual practice recognized women's contributions to culture and foregrounded women as subjects of some of the most important processes by which the community guaranteed its continuing welfare.«[120]

---

[120] Ibid, p.4

V. THE WORLD UPSIDE-DOWN

Theorizing Carnival: the Grotesque Realism of a Social Ritual

From the time of the Winter Solstice, December 21, with the sun lowest in the sky (the Christian Christmas) to the period of the Spring Equinox, March 21 (the Christian Easter) is when most of the world's festivals occur

In Northern Europe is the Goddess/God of Ice or death who must be placated in her Palace of the Midnight Sun; sacrifice will ensure the Spring. In the riverain & valleylands of what wd become the great Euro-nation-states, the concern settled in a wide arc from Equinox to Equinox, Autumn to Spring, giving us the great Ossirian/Orphic tales, the Harvest festivals, kites, scarecrowns, ships of Arthurian & Yseult death & desperado Carnival before the winter penance

In Amerindia, where the Gods of Sky & Wind had to be specially spoken to, the Solstice meant pumpkin, corn, bean (stalk) shored in before the Artic Circle takes over & so the icons of the festival were pumpkin, corn & bean (stalk) on the great circle of the cosmos

In India Maha-Kali, Nitya-Kali, Shmashana-Kali, Raksha-Kali, Shyma-Kali the Black One the festivals are mainly light & spring (flowers & animal & fruit) and water (moon/monsoon) axled again upon the solstices: Onam, Durga Puja (does Lakshmi carry on her head a crown or ancient galleon?) Dussehra & Divali [...]

In Africa, ancestral matrix of most of the Caribbean people that this book celebrates, this period is marked by Harmattan (& for the Moslems, Ramadan; & for the Hebrews, Habraham): the winter solstice bringing in the 'moving of the desert', great waves of sand drifting out of that ocean's centre to affect the Nile, the Rift Valley, the central lakes & west through SeneGambia & Ghana & Nigeria & west across Atlantic on the slave trade winds to Guanahani, Caribbean & beyond/ with the loveliest crimson sunset of drought

In all these cultures the ritual & iconography start with food [...] & vegetation: konkie & Pitchy-Patchy; & then as god of food & vegetation in the chain of being: man, yam, nyam, nyame, nam (to give it only one

> cultural nomen.clature) & then, esp in Africa & Amerindian, the mask of human/animal & the masks of god- kachina & konnu-&- in all-community-in need of reassurance/resurrection & survival ('fertility rites') entering the yearly crisis of the Winter Solstice: Divali, Dioula, Passover, Muharram, Christmas/Easter, Powamu, Chworu, Homowo
> [...]
>
> Carnival, wherever it occurs, is a crucial link in the chain of being. Its weakest link in a way, since it marks the community's moment of cr.sis when the river will rise when the monsoon will swoom when the locusts will swarm when the desert will quail when the lightning will kill. At that moment there will occur that twin (ibeji) &/or contradict.tory ritual of sacrifice & festival: the bacchanalian drinking of the split/split blood: the communal eating of the dismembered god & his/her reconstitution through & into the elements. into a new cycle of renewal/resurrection/ascension or groundation when the cosmos is re/turned to the ancestors are re/turned to the community is re/tur.ned to the living is re/turned to the elements is re/turned to the cosmos & that happy resolution is the carnival & the konnus are like gold or green or silver links of spirit of this rain.«[121]
> (E. Kamau Brathwaite, Alarms of God-Konnu and carnival in the Caribbean)

The origin of carnival is still doubtful, and therefore it has become a frequently debated subject. Thus, its roots reach back to five thousand years and more, and its vestige, which echoes traditions related to the evolution of the Egyptian cult of Isis, the goddess of fertility, to Greek worship of Dionysus and the Bacchanalia, the roman Lupercalia and Saturnalia, make Carnival one of the most ancient pagan festivities.

Carnival as we know it today, is, indeed, the result of a process of assimilation promoted by the catholic church after the end of the roman empire, that adjusted and permuted all the pre existing pagan festivities (which, in their turn, were the fruit of a continuous mutual exchange and hybridisation between different kinds of populations, their uses and customs and as a consequence of frequent wars of conquest, establish-

---

[121] Brathwaite, Kamau (1990): »Alarms of God-Konnu and Carnival in the Caribbean«, Caribbean quarterly vol. 36, nos. 3&4, special issue, Konnu and Carnival-Caribbean festival arts, University of the West Indies, Kingstone Jamaica, pp. 84-91

ment of new reigns, and mercantile traffics) in a new religious calendar.

According to Monica Rector, »Carnival is a pagan festivity with a Christian flavour«[122]; it is, in fact, the result of the legalization of the gaiety, misrule and laughter which characterized the ancient agricultural, propitiatory rites of fertility, actuated by the official church ideology. Florens C. Rang (Rang 1974) traced the origin of Carnival back to the Babylonians, who used to re-create a sanctioned upside down and chaotic »*interregnum*«, in order to »fill up« the gap in the calendar, that is, when the orbits of the moon (seasonal time) could not be rhythmically connected with the solar ones (normative time). Moreover, in antiquity, calendrical rites occurred periodically and predictably, accompanying seasonal changes in light, weather, agricultural work, and other social activities, giving socially meaningful definitions to the passage of time, creating an ever-renewing cycle of days, months, and years.

The flow of the time, the year, with the succession of the seasons, and its phases marked by the moon's and the sun's cycles, provided the frame of this order, to which the natural elements and the socially determined human being are both subjected: the cyclical rebirth of the nature, life and death, the old and the new, happiness and sadness, become all part of this particular time, which beats the time of our existence. Therefore, the use of various intercalary days to coordinate the lunar or solar calendars ensures a correspondence between the ritual occasion and a particular time of the year, which often evokes a rich set of associations between the seasons of nature and the rhythm of social life. Carnival, is the »break«, astrologically and symbolically speaking, which follows the fall of the old year's star and the epiphany of the new year's (that covers a period of time of three months, between January and March); it is, indeed a procession, which is materialized in the cortege of jubilant people following a *carrus navalis* that will guide them to a new and safe shore.

---

122 Rector, Monica: »Code and Message of Carnival«, in Eco, Umberto/Ivanov V., V/Rector, Monica (1984): »Carnival!, Approaches to Semiotics«, Mouton Publishers, Berlin, New York, Amsterdam, p. 38

Whether it was the masquerade procession following the *carrus navalis* on its way to the Nile in Iside's honour; the one characterized by the frenetic and ecstatic dances of the Bacchae, with their faces painted with blackberry and grape juice (Rang 1974), and Satiris paying homage with the entire community in invoking the protection of the gods and in offering thanksgiving for the abundance, in a licentious mood; or the Roman's Saturnalia, where the slaves used to be crowned masters, as the satiric figure who was elected king for a day and then dethroned at the end of the festivity, all of these contributed to the medieval carnival marking the onset of the Christian fast, becoming »the people's second life, organized on the basis of laughter [...] the true feast of time, the feast of becoming, change and renewal. It was hostile to all it was immortalized and complete«[123] Christian culture was, indeed, an admirable blend of sacred and profane, religious and burlesque.

In terms of etymology, the word Carnival, although its origins are nowadays still dubious, probably derives from the Medieval Latin *carne levamen*, later modified *carne, vale!* (farewell to meat), indicating a day of gustatory excess before the Lenten deprivation, since carnival is a libratory pre-Lenten festivity, that has its climax during the three days before Ash Wednesday. Although these religious notions are pertinent and give the spatial and temporal frame to carnival itself, they do not describe and justify completely Carnival's content, meaning, and function. In fact, according to David Gilmore:

»Like nature, society reveals nothing, certainly not its deepest secrets, without ceremonies. [...] The secrets in question are those which affect the people deeply and shape their social relations: secrets about sex, gender and status.«[124]

Thus carnival rhetoric within its madcap ritual context has much to tell us about how people experience and perceive their society and its traditions as elements of the conscious life. These festivals involve certain highly marked symbolic inversions of

---

[123] Bakhtin, Mikhail (1984): »Rabelais and His World«, Indiana University Press, Bloomington, pp. 8-10
[124] Gilmore (1998): op. cit, p. 1

identity and aspects of behaviours that characterize the everyday life of the communities and their members. Carnival, in fact, beside its formal aspect of an occasion for maximum social chaos and licentious play, may be considered particularly ritualistic because it draws together many social groups who are normally kept separate and create specific times and places where social differences are either laid aside or reversed for a more embracing experience of community.

The inversion and license of festival should be approached in terms of the general inter-relationship between order and disorder in the moral and social universe of the communities in which rite of reversal are conducted, for it is not simply a celebratory event that is bound in time and space, but also the source of a popular culture which infiltrates official culture, permeating it with humour, irony and indeterminacy. On this regard, Barbara Babcock asserts:

»If there is a given in these discussions it is that man both orders and disorders his environment and his experience. [...] Such »creative negations« remind us of the need to reinvest the clean with the filthy, the rational with the animalistic, the ceremonial with the carnivalesque in order to maintain cultural vitality. And they confirm the endless potentiality of dirt and the pure possibility of liminality. The mundus inversus does more than simply mock our desire to live according to our usual orders and norms; it reinvests life with a vigor and a Spielraum attainable (it would seem) no other way. The process of symbolic inversion, far from being a residual category of experience, is its very opposite. What is socially peripheral is often symbolically central, and if we ignore or minimize inversion and other forms of cultural negation we often fail to understand the dynamics of symbolic processes generally.«[125]

The general theory of carnival as an inversion of binary oppositions was principally outlined by the Russian Michael Bakhtin, who popularized the idea of carnival as a signifier of joyful relativism- a »temporary liberation from the prevailing truth

---

[125] Babcock, Barbara, A. (edited by) (1978): »The Reversible World, Symbolic inversion in art and society«, Cornell University Press, Ithaca and London, pp. 31-32

and from the established order«[126] that emphasizes ambivalence, or the unfinalizability of life.

Carnival is a festive expression that deforms, deconstructs, reinterprets the world as it is in various ways, for its sense of the world »permeating these serious –comic genres from the top to the bottom, determines their basic features and places image and word in them in a special relationship to reality...there is a weakening of its one sided theoretical seriousness, its rationality, it singular meaning, its rationalism [...]«.[127] Carnival's *Mundus inversus* generates a new range of imagery; everything known to us can be shown in systematically altered relationships.

Carnival is the language of the market place crowd, the folk language, the one dialectically contra posed to the official monologue; it uses a set of symbols which may have much in common with a grosser, absurd, topsy-turvy popular imagery that Bakhtin calls the grotesque realism:

»[...] the carnival grotesque form exercises the same function: to consecrate inventive freedom, to permit the combination of a variety of different elements and their reapprocement, to liberate from the prevailing point of view of the world, from conventions and established truths, from clichés, from all that is humdrum and universally accepted. This carnival spirit offers the chance to have a new outlook on the world, to realize the relative nature of all that exists, and to enter a completely new order of things.«[128]

There are several debates between the scholars regarding the socio political carnival; on one hand most of the work so far adheres to the »safety valve« model (following the wake of Gluckman's theory on ritual of rebellion), in which the exuberance of carnival is seen as a letting off of steam among the masses, its excess, for instance, was encouraged as a religious pedagogic device to drive home to the people their inherent inclination to vices of excess in order to turn them more effectively to the purifying asceticism of Lent.

---

126 Bakhtin (1984): op. cit, p. 10
127 Ibid, p. 92
128 Ibid, p. 34

According to Umberto Eco, carnival is an instrument of social control, aimed to »support the universe of business, there is no business like show business«[129]. By assuming that »the idea of carnival has something to do with comic«, he asserts that: »comic is only an instrument of social control and can never be a form of social criticism«[130], for its cathartic impact is socially conservative. The comic effect, in fact, is realized when:

»1 there is a violation of a rule (preferably, but not necessarily, a minor one, like an etiquette rule); 2 the violation is committed by someone with whom we do not sympathize because he is an ignoble, inferior and repulsive (animal-like) character; 3 therefore we feel superior to his misbehaviour and to his sorrow for having broken the rule; 4 however in recognizing that the rule has been broken, we do not feel concerned; on the contrary we in some way welcome the violation; we are, so to speak, revenged by the comic character who has challenged the repressive power of the rule (which involves no risk to us, since we commit the violation only vicariously); 5 our pleasure is a mixed one because we enjoy not only the breaking of the rule but also the disgrace of an animal-like individual; 6 at the same time we are neither concerned with the defence of the rule nor compelled toward compassion for such an inferior being.«[131]

The audience laugh at the predicament of the comic characters, while feeling a sense of relief at the break of the rule, and, at the same time, a sense of superiority that negate the audience to sympathize and develop a sense of unity with them. Thus in the comedy, as in carnival, there must be rules and rituals to be parodied. Carnival, indeed, according to Eco exists only as an authorized transgression (Eco/Ivanov/Rector 1984). Barbara Babcock explains that:

»The world order of any culture is in great part determined not only by the things, event or actions put into order, but by those acts, events, and anomalous things which exhibit disorderliness, chaos and filth. [...]

---

129 Eco, Umberto: »The Frames of Comic 'Freedom'«, in Eco/Ivanov/Rector: op.cit, p. 3
130 Ibid, p. 7
131 Ibid, p. 3

Similarly, the social interaction system involves both the conventional means of articulating orders and rules and the counteractive patterns by which those very conventions may be profitably and recognizably transformed.

An especially important form of symbolic inversion is that used to mark a boundary, between peoples, between categories of persons, between life and death.

This means that a group membership is determined not only by what members share, but by what the members recognize that »significant others« do not share.

Thus developing the notions of stereotyping and deviance: the definition of those outsider »on the periphery« in terms of how they depart from insider to the direction of nature or chaos (violation of the social order).«[132]

The closed systems of social status and prestige that are put on public display in these particular carnival traditions do not simply illustrate the tensions between elitism and populism but also literally perform them; for these reasons, some scholars argue that rituals like carnival can help to change the status quo, while others suggest that they actually work to reinforce it. Thus, what Turner called social drama provides, in the form of religious plays, passion plays or carnival festivities, an insight of a different kind into the complexity of the dialectic relationship between ritual and social structure; that is, that the upside-down world of Carnival often acts as a form of protest against the existing social structure and contributes to social change. In fact, these collective traditions may give rise to dramatic forms that are intensely critical and even experimental in their representation of social and political structure.

Carnival and its accompanying components represent a theory of resistance, a theory of freedom from all domination. For the fact that popular festivities were closely related forms of social life, neighbouring institutions with similar patterns of representation and similar orientations to political and economic practice, Carnival may be considered »the place for working out a new mode of interrelationship between individuals«[133].

---

132   Babcock, op. cit, p. 27
133   Bakhtin (1984): op. cit, p. 123

Yet as the work of Bakhtin reminds us, there was always an inherent possibility of unofficial subversion of authority and hierarchy through the alternative potential of the 'culture of laughter'. Carnival, indeed, exemplified the complex and subtle dialectic between the official and the unofficial, it is, according to David Gilmore, »this dialectic of culture and counter culture that endlessly renegotiates tradition«[134].

According to Bakhtin, Carnival is an important primary form of human culture, because of its power to shape a complete world with its own space and time by reflecting and deconstructing wider social and political concerns such as class and gender divisions. Thus, Carnival is a complex cultural and social phenomenon, which is based on an interrelationship of various codes (musical, verbal visual, gestural), whose actions form a pattern of symbols that dramatize shared values and beliefs concerning the world in which people live. Victor Turner pointed out that:

»if the daily living is a kind of theatre, social drama is a kind of metatheatre, that is a dramaturgical language about the language of ordinary role playing and status maintenance which constitutes communication in the quotidian social process.«[135]

This set of symbols, in fact, represents a *metalanguage* that:

»[...] enable participants and spectators to realize just how far they have fallen short of or transgressed their own ideal standards, or even, in some kind of ritual, to call those very rituals into question under conditions of sharp social change.«[136]

Although Bakhtin argues that popular inversive rituals are never purely parodies, for the popular imagination is never bare, nor ambiguous (»the spirit of carnival denies but it revives

---

134 Gilmore (1998): op. cit, p. 210
135 Turner (1986): op. cit., p. 76
136 Turner, Victor (1979): »Frame Flow and Reflection, Ritual Drama as Public Liminality«, Japanese Journal of Religious Studies 4/6, December, p. 467

and renews at the same time bare negation is completely alien to folk culture«[137]), the nature of carnival is ambivalent.

On one hand folk culture appears periodically as a culture of laughter by means of an ensemble of rites and symbols, of a temporarily existing life form that enables carnival to take place, on the other the principle of laughter which organizes carnival, is universal and transtemporal. Carnival, indeed, is social and antisocial, conservative and progressive, universal and specific, as Bakhtin asserted:

»[...] it is universal in scope; it is directed at all and everyone, including the carnival partecipants. The entire world is seen in its droll aspects, in its gay relativity [...] this laughter is ambivalent: it is gay, triumphant and at the same time mocking, deriding. It asserts and denies, it buries and revives. Such is the laughter of Carnival.«[138]

Bakhtin´s dialogic world is inherently responsive, involving individuals acting at particular points in time and space, in reaction to what has gone before and in expectation of what is to follow. In other words, as Turner would say, Carnival is the dialectic between »is« and »may be«, it is the subjuntive mood of a communitas, which through action (performance/ acting out) the ideal of a community, is capable of being reflective and reflexive at the same time, creating the experience of the community, by arousing consciousness of ourselves as we see ourselves. Cultural performances like Carnival might be:

»not simple mirrors but magical mirrors of social reality: they exaggerate, invert, reform, magnify, minimize, discolor, recolor, even deliberately falsify, chronicled events.«[139]

So the peculiarity of Carnival cannot be its aesthetic impact (that is the first visual impression on the performance which might make us laugh) on the spectators, but its political and societal matter, since this festival is strictly correlated with the reality of a community and only as such can maintain its original nature. The subversive logic of carnival and its grotesque real-

---

137 Bakhtin (1984): op. cit., p. 11
138 Ibid, pp. 11-12
139 Turner (1986): op. cit., p. 42

ity are seen as the folk consciousness of the power and the possibility to shape their own future, that is, of the fact that each man belongs to the »immortal people who create history«[140].

---

[140] Bakhtin (1984): op. cit., p. 367

VI. THE AMBIVALENCE OF TRINIDAD CARNIVAL. MUSIC, MASKING AND PERFORMANCE: THE »MAGICAL MIRROR« OF A HYBRID SOCIETY

»All o' we is one«: Carnival as a Symbol of National Identity and Unity

> »For nearly three centuries there was no place for art, or the artist, in West Indian society. It is doubtful whether any other culture of which we have any records has ever focussed its energies with such singlemindedness of purpose into the one channel of commercial exploitation. For nearly three centuries the West Indian thought nothing, created nothing, explored nothing. If at any time, between Columbus and the Second World War the British Caribbean Islands had sunk beneath the sea, the world would have lost little that enriches the imagination of mankind.
>
> This was a condition imposed on us by history, by social conflicts too enormous for us to discuss here but which generated a society unique in its inarticulate sterility. All societies are bound to a cycle of labour for profitable production; all societies, except the West Indian, use some part of those profits to sustain the arts.
>
> And yet the West Indies of today is not the brutishly philistine territory which was fashioned on the sugar plantations of the past. It is a society so eager to define itself, so conscious of suddenly released energies, that the dialogue is often incoherent. It probably writes too much, paints too much, dances too much, asks for too much too soon. When the political dam broke every sensitive man and woman realized that we lacked, in Yeats'great phrase, 'that unity from a mythology that marries us to rock and hill'.«[141]
>
> (John Hearne, The Artists of West Indian Society)

---

[141] In: Hill, Errol (edited by) (1963): »The Artists in West Indian Society, a Symposium«, Department of Extra-Mural Studies, University of West Indies.

Although there is a shared past behind the West Indies concerning diverse social, geographical, economical and historical aspects, the history, culture and social composition of each island is dissimilar. In fact, European conquest, slavery, the plantation economy, and the immigration had a different background and effect in each country. Thus, West Indian performances, languages, social assumptions, music, etc have been influenced by a diverse context, and therefore there is a past and present identity needing to be told through many different perspectives and voices.

Considering that all cultures are intercultural and transnational (Bhabha 1994) and participate in an ongoing exchange with others, with elite and popular forms, in the process of creating and revitalizing their own identity according to their time, place, actualities, desires, and needs, that is to say that the creative and imaginative vitality of the West Indies derives mainly from its different genes, cultures, histories and problems.

One of the best models to understand Caribbean culture and society is carnival, for it is a distinctive blend of many cultures, differences, histories and people, while remaining Caribbean and having its origin in a particular time and place. Caribbean culture is the result of a syncretism that comes from the relationship among several human groups of different origin and from various types of cultural creativity.

Secular festivals, like carnival, are derived from pre-colonial traditions which have been altered in response to changing circumstances and contexts. Because of the tendency of being relatively open in structure, these festivals often become highly syncretic events which incorporate many elements of colonising culture even while expressing difference and/or dissent from them. Most of these secular festivals are rooted in cyclical and calendar rituals in which the whole collective participates. At certain moments of the seasonal cycle, which are defined differently in various cultures, certain groups or categories of people, usually occupying an inferior position, exercise ritual authority over their superiors by establishing a hierarchy that resembles a parody of the normal hierarchical order of the superiors.

The political dimension of the ritual intersects with the sacred, not least because many rituals were officially banned by imperial agents. Such forbidden events became subversive activities under colonial rule and can now function as symbols of liberty for an independent post-colonial system, especially when ritual is contextualized by or located in a particular community. Thus, all cultural practices (like theatre or secular festival) informed by ritual aim to do more than merely keep the spectator aesthetically engaged; ritual, in fact, is a central way of transforming and simultaneously maintaining the spiritual and the common health of a society. Ritual based traditional enactments do not remain static but transform to fit the contingencies of the new context; and in Trinidad (Caribbean) one of the most obvious and prominent of these transformations of cultural signifiers has been Carnival.

The Trinidad Carnival is by far the most significant festival in Trinidad and Tobago. It has evolved over the past two centuries from an elegant, exclusive affair to a truly all-inclusive national festival. Indeed, as Errol Hill clearly pointed out, Trinidadian Carnival is:

»[...] not simply a retention of an European inspired festival. It may resemble in many characteristic ways the carnivals of other countries, but its ancestry is different: in Trinidad the carnival underwent a complete metamorphosis, a rebirth, resulting from peculiar historical and social pressures of the early 19th century. The effect of this metamorphosis was to make the Trinidad carnival essentially a local product in form, content, and inner significance.«[142]

Although carnival was introduced in Trinidad at the end of the 18th century by the French planters' elite and had incorporated elements from the European culture, it had managed, throughout the history of Caribbean people and their becoming an independent nation, to re-interpret traditions belonging to an African past. In fact, Carnival in Trinidad and Tobago originally had its roots in West African festivals, facilitated by the conservative French aristocracy's carnival celebrations (fancy mas-

---

142 Hill, Errol (1997): »The Trinidad Carnival: Mandate for a National Theatre«, University of Texas, Austin, p. 5

querade balls, house to house visits...) that brought to the island the »legacy of carnival«[143].

Throughout human history, this complex secular cultural expression has undergone several transformations and contaminations, dating from its origins as a pagan festivity (for example by the Greeks), inherited then by the Romans, transformed in the Middle Ages in a goliardic festival with a Christian flavour, promoted to masked balls by French and Italian nobles in the Renaissance (Venetian Carnival), brought from the French colonisers overseas to, finally, its implication in the post emancipation process of »cultural re-birth and construction of a new national identity« of the former colonies. Thus, according to Errol Hill:

»Since the first masquerade held in pre-Christian times, carnival has exhibited recognizable features wherever it has taken roots and flourished. Clearly originating in a worship of a nature deity- whether the Egyptian Isis, the Greek Dionysus, the Roman Saturn, or some other is immaterial- carnival proceedings have included street processions, costuming and masking, music making, energetic dancing, singing of satiric or laudatory songs, jesting, mummery, feasting, and general revelry. Specific practices that have survived over centuries are torch carrying, bonfire lighting (originally aimed at purifying the fields and frightening off demons, thereby ensuring a good crop), and pitched battles between contesting bands symbolic of the struggle between Life and Death, Summer and Winter, New Year and Old Year, or the more mystic combat between the forces of Good and Evil. Among the earliest characters impersonated at these festivities and still associated with carnivals are demons (in a variety of shapes and dresses) the clown or buffoon, and the transvestite.

When the Roman Catholic Church adopted carnival as a pre-Lenten festival, it gave religious sanction to a pagan rite too profoundly rooted in the sustenance of life to be effectively suppressed. Church warrant, however, did not change the festival in any of its significant forms, but had the effect of spreading the observance of carnival to those countries,

---

143 Hollis, Urban, Liverpool (1998): »Origins of Rituals and Customs in the Trinidad Carnival: African or European?«, TDR Vol. 42, No.3, Trinidad and Tobago Carnival, August 1998, p. 4

including several in the new world, where the roman church held sway as the dominant religion. In this way carnival came to Trinidad.«[144]

Over the last two centuries, carnival has been transformed from an elegant and exclusive affair, formally introduced by the French planters settled in Trinidad by the Cedula of Population in 1783, into what is called the greatest show on earth.

The present day carnival is the result of an ongoing process of hybridizations, adaptations, evolutions and cultural persistence, by mirroring from different angles a society whose search for a social integration continues to struggle with its pluralist tendencies dictated by a history of fragmentations, abuses of power and its inevitable consequences. In fact, as Milla Cozart Riggio wrote: »the history of Trinidad Carnival is essentially the history of the peoples of Trinidad- embedded in the stories of conquest, enslavement, resistance, and indentureship, and in commercial, cultural, and ethnic exchange among the many who were forcibly brought to the place or settled there […].«[145].

The pre-emancipation festival period was characterized by the absolute presence of the French elite and its customs. The festivities were reserved for the privileged white class, while the free persons of colour could have worn masks, but were not allowed to join the amusements of the privileged (but they were allowed to have separate festivities), and the enslaved Africans were never allowed to take part at all. When, in 1797 the British took possession of the island, carnival tradition was already so deeply rooted in the population customs, that any efforts to constrain the event were in vain. Although the carnival celebrations between 1783 and 1838 were dominated by the white elite, and Africans and coloureds were forbidden by law to participate in the (public) festivities, although they did celebrate in their own way in their compounds. In fact, according to Andrew Pearse:

---

144 Hill (1997): op. cit,. p. 5
145 Riggio, Cozart, Milla: »The Carnival Story- Then and Now«, in Riggio Cozart Milla (edited by) (2004): »Carnival Culture in Action the Trinidad Experience«, Routledge, New York and London, p. 39

»Carnival enables all the non-slave population to adopt fictitious social roles, and, indeed, in masking on the street at least, to overstep the social boundaries of colour. [...]
The slaves were excluded from Carnival, but whether in African, or in Creole and European style were universally given licence at Christmas time, for dancing, feasting at the master's expense, some freedom of movement, and elaborate costuming.«[146]

The events following the Emancipation in 1838 have been forging gradually what was going to become this fascinating and contradictory cultural expression of folk pride, national identity, and eventually an exportable product. According to Bridget Brereton, »the last three decades of the 18th century were crucial years for the development of Trinidad Carnival«[147], for it was the time when the black population took possession of the streets, and carnival turned into what Fraser called »a noisy and disorderly amusement for the lower classes« (quoted by Andrew Pearse 1988)[148]. Carnival was, in fact, entirely taken over by the *Jammette*- that is the *diamatres* (Brereton 1975), the »underworld« class of Port of Spain- becoming an arena »in which class antagonism were worked out«, for it was the Bakhtian model of reversal »of all the values and judgements of a respectable society«[149].

The carnival of the post-emancipation period developed into an annual ritual of social protest and resistance by the African population against the hegemony of the European elite. The former slave selected to celebrate their newly won freedom in carnivalesque style, by reproducing or enacting the *cannes brules* or *Canboulay* procession (a torchlight procession which was a ceremonial re-enactment of the gang of slaves mustered late at night to put out cane fires) (Brereton 1975) on the night of August 1, the date of the emancipation; they also ran out onto the

---

146 Pearse, Andrew (c1988): »Carnival in 19th Century Trinidad, in Trinidad Carnival«, Caribbean Quarterly Trinidad Carnival Issue, Vol.4 No 3&4, 1956, Paria, Port of Spain, Trinidad, p. 19
147 Brereton, Bridget (1975): »The Trinidad Carnival 1870-1900«, Savacou 11-12, Sept 1975, edited by the Caribbean Artists movement, Herald Ltd, Kingston, Jamaica, p. 46
148 Pearse: op. cit., p. 9
149 Brereton (1975): op. cit, p. 46

streets during carnival days, masquerading with explicit sexual themes, stickfighting, drumming, dancing, making indecent gestures and singing »lewd songs«, breaking the boundaries or respectability and colonial order.

Thus, on the streets, was displayed the essence of carnival, that is, the class conflicts performed as status inversion and proletarian rebellion against elitism and hierarchy, ridiculing authority and extolling an utopia of human equality as a political alternative in a mutual morally inversive and politically subversive way. Since then, for almost all the duration of the 19th century, the authorities and the middle class, that is the *superstructure* (Pearse 1988), started to withdraw the festival, making several attempts to abolish it, but to no avail. This climax reached its maximum apex of tension between 1881 and 1884, when the canboulay riots erupted against the Governor's control, consequently destroying the rapport between the police and the revellers.

During the subsequent years the Government eliminated the organized band warfare, suppressed some of the obviously obscene masks, and made canboulay illegal. Thus, while carnival continued to be celebrated (according to Milla Riggio »canboulay won out. Its Kalinda dance and its lavways established the basis for the modern Carnival«[150]), political pressure, in conjunction with middle- and upper-class resistance to the practice, kept it from gaining popular acceptance during the nineteenth century.

By the 1890s carnival was driven underground by a governmental »purging« policy, which led carnival becoming a festival acceptable to most sectors of society, including the upper and the middle class. Gradually the celebration became less controversial, and by the middle of the 20th century, was a reasonably well-accepted Trinidadian cultural marker. By the late 1970s, a growing patriotism began to draw Trinidadians toward re-identifying and re-appropriating those practices and symbols that might assist them in creating and maintaining a distinct cultural identity. As Peter Van Koningsbruggen asserted:

---

150 Riggio, Cozart, Milla (1998): »Introduction, Resistance and Identity«, TDR 1988, Vol.42, No.3, Trinidad and Tobago Carnival (Autumn 1998), p. 4

»The function of carnival as a national cultural event is the result of almost two centuries of history, in which specific events which were initially confined to specific social groups gradually became the common property of society at large and were transformed into national symbols. In a nutshell: what was at first a festival belonging to the sociocultural domain of the French Creole planter elite was transferred to that of the black lower class after the abolition of slavery (1834); with the increased interest and participation of the Creole middle class from the beginning of the twentieth century, it has turned into a festival of national importance.«[151]

It was during the search for unity and culturalism that Carnival was seized upon and rapidly pressed into service as a central and defining symbol of belonging to a new free (independent) nation. In fact, even though the population of Trinidad and Tobago is diverse, a national identity and national self-image was taking shape. These image characteristics sponsored by Carnival included pride in cultural diversity, vestiges from the British colonial heritage, and elements of creative resistance to British colonialism. On this concern Ngũgĩ wa Thiong'o explains that:

»The war between the art and the state is really a struggle between the power of performance in the arts and the performance of power by the state- in short, enactment of power. The conflict in the enactment of power is sharper where the state is externally imposed, in a situation where there is a conqueror and the conquered for instance, as in colonialism.«[152]

Rituals of reversals such as Carnival are characterized by articulated political ideologies that protest against the social and political status quo, which in certain circumstances, could lead to a proper revolt. In his analysis of the Carnival in Romans in 1580 Le Roy Ladurie demonstrated how the seasonal festival

---

151 Koningsbruggen Van, Peter (1997): »Trinidad Carnival A Quest for a National Identity«, Macmillan Education Ltd, London, p. 2
152 Ngũgĩ, wa, Thiong'o (1997): »Enactments of Power: The politics of Performance Space«, TDR 1988, Vol. 41 No.3, (Autumn 1997), The MIT Press, p. 12

was strictly endowed with the Parisian socio-political substructure (or antistructure, referring to Turner's terminology) of the 16th century, by asserting that:

»The Carnival in Romans made ready use of the reynages. It was rooted in the Paris confraternity-related culture of time. The notables and other leaders, great or small, plebeian or rich, wanted to épater les burgeois (to unsettle people). They pursued certain finalities, in some cases conservatives or radical one; they attained their goal by donating a modest sum of money or quantity of wax and becoming king for a few days during the carnival, Easter, or summer festivities.
Catholic culture under the ancient régime was an admirable blend of sacred and profane, religious and burlesque. In the reynage it had created a social tool, allowing the lower classes to express themselves, their mockery, and sometimes even their grievances. Plebeian political tendencies that were repressed during the rest of the year came to light during the festivities. A dangerous group subconscious found a temporary outward structuring in the solemn and formalized institutions of the reynage.«[153]

For Turner »liminality«, which is fully manifested (performed) in carnival, is the »realm of pure possibility« (Turner 1967), and may operate as a means of social control, of social protest, of social change, and of social deviance depending on the historical and social context. Thus ritual, by redressing the limitations of the social structure have a politically integrative role, which, in the industrialized societies, may be part of the process of social change. Consequently, the subversive character of Carnival might be related to what Karl Marx wrote of the proletarian revolution:

»Proletarian revolutions, on the other hand, like those of the 19th century, criticise themselves constantly, interrupt themselves continually in their own course, come back to the apparently accomplished in order to begin it afresh, deride with unmerciful thoroughness the inadequacies, weaknesses and paltrinesses of their first attempts, seem to throw down their adversary only in order that he may draw new strength from the

---

153 Le Roy, Ladurie (1981): »Carnival in Romans, a people's uprising at Romans 1579-1580«, Penguin Books, Middlesex, p. 282

earth and rise again more gigantic before them, recoil ever and anon from the indefinite prodigiousness of their own aims, until the situation has been created which makes all turning back impossible, and the conditions themselves cry out:
Hic Rhodus, hic salta!
Hier ist die Rose, hier tanze!
(here is the rhodes, leap here, here is the Rose, dance here« the words are from a fable by Aesop about a braggart who claimed he could produce witnesses to prove he had once made a remarkable leap in Rhodes, to which claim he received the reply: »Why cite witnesses, if it is true? Here is the Rhodes, leap here« that is »show us right here what you can do«. The German paraphrase of the Greek quotation (Rhodus means rose) was used by Hegel in the preface to his philosophy of Right)«[154]

Since Carnival in Trinidad is the fruit of local and global histories, and the changing within these settings, -Spanish, British and French colonialism; the plantation system, slavery indentured servitude, the international markets for sugar, cocoa, and oil; and anticolonial agitation, decolonization, and the vicissitudes of state and nation formation after independence, it has become both the reflection and the main expression of the entire society, nation and culture.

For a better and deeper understanding of political and cultural realities of the Caribbean area, it is of primary importance to consider the British colonial practice of »divide –and –rule« as relevant in promoting class and racial divisions within the subordinate populations, and in yielding the consequences that in the post-independent Caribbean have become manifested in the region's political culture.

The race and class inequalities, that were so crucial to the stability and effectiveness of colonial rule, have mutated into the contemporary period, and although the colonizers are no longer present, the political consciousness of the wider population continues to be divided on race and class criteria. Caribbean political culture has been always (and it still does) mirror-

---

[154] Marx, Karl: »The Eighteenth Brumaire of Louis Bonaparte«, in Tucker, Robert, C. (1978): »The Marx-Engel Reader«, W.W Norton & Company, Princeton University, p. 597

ing this debate over race and class, albeit under changed circumstances.

In order to achieve a whole independence, Caribbean people had to reject the colonizers' definition; whereas being »black« and African were once the symbols of mental/cultural inferiority and impotence, in the lead-up to independence, black people began to invert that understanding of themselves and to proclaim pride in and derive strength from their colour and ancestral land. Therefore, although the problem toward West Indian independence was multiracial, because of the black and brown majority of the region and the social cleavages of colonialism, the formal political independence had to be »black in complexion«.

On the other hand, one of the crucial dimensions of identity is national identity, which basically is the cultural relationship between the individual and the collectivity, understood through territoriality. In fact, territory and culture can endow people with myths and symbols of unique identity; and cultural phenomena, above all, remain the dominant social bond par excellence. As Eric Hobsbawm explains:

»[...] the state linked both formal and informal, official and unofficial, political and social inventions of tradition, at least in those countries where the need for it arose. [...]
It was thus natural that the classes within society, and in particular the working class, should tend to identify themselves through nationalwide political movements or organizations ('parties'), and equally natural that, de facto these should operate essentially within the confines of the nation. Nor it is surprising that movements seeking to represent an entire society or 'people' should envisage its existence essentially in terms of that of an independent or at least an autonomous state. State, nation and society converged.«[155]

Thus, according to Ernest Gellner, »the cultural shreds and patches used by nationalism are often arbitrary historical inven-

---

155 Hobsbawm, Eric: »The Nation an Invention of Tradition«, in Hutchinson John/ Smith, Anthony, D., (edited by) (1994): »Nationalism«, Oxford University Press, Oxford, New York, pp. 76-77

tions«[156]. In the Caribbean the process of nation building was complex and ambivalent, for it responded to the needs of both contrasting the imposed society structure and division, and of creating a new nation to which the different ethnic groups equally belonged and could identify with. The »idea« of nation, then, had to be »truly Caribbean«.

Karl Marx asserted, explaining the mechanisms of the 19th century proletarian revolutions, that:

»Men make their own history, but they do not make it just as they please; they do not make it under circumstances chosen by themselves, but under circumstances directly found, given and transmitted from the past. The tradition of all the dead generations weighs like a nightmare on the brain of the living. And just when they seem engaged in revolutionizing themselves and things, in creating something entirely new, precisely in such epochs of revolutionary crisis they anxiously conjure up the spirits of the past to their service and borrow from them names, battle slogans, and costumes in order to present the new scene of the world history in this time-honoured disguise and this borrowed language. [...]
In like the manner the beginner who has learnt a new language always translates it back into his mother tongue, but he has assimilated the spirit of the new language and can produce freely in it only when he moves in it without remembering the old and forgets in it his ancestral tongue.«[157]

Since the idea of the nation is often based on naturalized myths of racial and cultural origin, the need to assert such myths was a vital part of the collective cultural resistance and nation building, which focused on issues of separate identity and cultural distinctiveness from the past colonial heritage.

Many different factors have been involved in giving form to the Caribbean nationalism. Of a great influence was the way in which racial categories have taken form in the region. The island territories of the Caribbean have been multiracial societies

---

156 Gellner, Ernest (1983): »Nations and Nationalism«, Blackwell, Oxford, Basil, p. 56
157 Marx, Karl: »The Eighteenth Brumaire of Louis Bonaparte«, in Tucker: op. cit, p. 595

since their incorporation into the capitalistic world system very early in the sixteenth century.

The way collective identities have developed in this part of the world has been affected by this multiracial background. Thus syncretism, as opposed to nativism (in the same way as blackness was an antithesis to whiteness and Britishness) on one hand and assimilation to the other, was the basis for the generation of a new Caribbean culture, the bearer of a new Caribbean nationality.

In the Caribbean, nationalist movements were characterized by two main features: on one hand it was expressed in racial identities that transcended any particular territory, idealizing Africa as the land of the Ancestors; on the other, it stressed the civic and territorial characteristics with the ethnic qualities of a shared culture. Indeed the pursuit of the new Caribbean middle class was to create a pure Caribbean black identity which could symbolically bind the diverse ethnic groups, by constructing an ideal and utopic imagined community based on the myth of racial democracy. As a direct expression of the folk and, in a true sense, belonging to the black lower class, Carnival reflected all these expectations, becoming instrumentally constitutive of the shared imaginary sponsored by the dominant culture.

Carnival for Bakhtin is both a populist utopian vision of the world seen from below and a festive critique, through the inversion of hierarchy, of the high culture. Carnival is presented by Bakhtin as a world of topsy-turvy, where all is mixed, hybrid, ritually degraded and defiled. However, it is striking that the most successful of these attempts to apply Bakhtin tout court, focus upon cultures which still have a strong repertoire of carnivalesque practices, such as the West Indies, where the political difference between the dominant and subordinate culture is particularly charged. On this regard, the theatre theorist Richard Schechner asserts that:

»Bakhtin's notions of carnival are founded on a settled, stratified society -a non-democratic society. In such a setting, authority can be suspended or set aside temporarily, and »the people« given a chance to act out their desires freely if temporarily. But today's world is not that kind of world. In the places where carnival as a formal institution is performed (Trinidad and Tobago, New Orleans Mardi Gras, and Rio de Janeiro, for example), the social »baseline« is democracy or the illusion of democracy. It is not that »the people« really have power on a daily basis or ultimately. But from time to time there are elections in which »the people« are appealed to, their votes sought, bought, and manipulated. This kind of democracy is both dysfunctional (in the US, nearly half the eligible voters do not vote) and illusory. The image-makers provide a daily diet of patriotism linked to democracy. But even if untrue, the »make believe« of democracy depends on the psychosocial phenomenon that »the people« are sovereign.«[158]

Thus Carnival might be considered as a cultural phenomenon which »reflects local society in the same way that modern art responds to civilization: in both, the depiction of unspeakable reality can be passed off as idiosyncratic, subjective, deviant, tolerable under carefully circumscribed conditions«.[159] The public displaying, then, must be seen as a politically significant mise-en-scène, where the energy and initiative of the collective life are forcefully manifested in texts, in performance convention, and in the audience's reception and appreciation. Throughout the Caribbean colonial history, carnival became a resource of actions, images and roles which may be invoked to legitimate desire; it is, indeed, the public »unmasking« of the Others, whose consequence is:

»[...] mobile, conflictual fusion of power, fear and desire in the construction of subjectivity: a psychological dependence upon precisely those Others which are being rigorously opposed and excluded at the social level. It is for this reason that what is socially peripheral is so frequently symbolically central.«[160]

---

158 Schechner, Richard: »Carnival (Theory) After Bakhtin«, in Riggio (2004): op. cit., p. 3
159 Guillotte, Joseph, V.: »Every Man a King: reflection on the aesthetics of ritual rebellion in Mardi Gras Plantation society«, in Fierher, Thomas, M./ Lodwick, Michael, W. (edited by) (1990): »Plantation Society in the Americas- Carnival in Perspective, An Interdisciplinary Journal of Tropical and Subtropical History and Culture«, Popular Press, Bowling Green, Ohio, pp. 43-44
160 Stallybrass, Peter/White, Allon (1986): »The Politics and Poetics of Transgression«, Methuen & Co. Ltd, London, p. 5

Trinidad Carnival is no longer the ludic inversion, the steam valve, which characterized carnivals in the medieval Europe, since it may be more appropriate to describe it as »magical mirror« (Turner 1986), that is, a: »'ritual of intensification' (Nancy Scheper Hughes »Death without weeping« 1992: 482; quoted by Richard D.E Burton) in which the forces that govern 'ordinary' life are expressed with a particular salience, clarity and eloquence.«[161]. Carnival is, in fact, a festival warranting year round discussions, preparations and anticipation, »where any event takes a nation over so completely or so neatly brings together so many aspects of its culture, of its strengths and weakness. [...]

It is an all year-round statement of identity. [...] In other countries carnival is a diversion from the troubles of life; in Trinidad it sometimes seems as if life is a diversion from carnival.«[162]

The history of Trinidad Carnival over the last two and half centuries was characterized by the evolution music, song, dance, mime and masquerade that have made it a grand theatrical spectacle and repository of the nation's performing arts.

Carnival is the interrelationship of four main codes: the verbal, the visual, the musical and the gestural, which in Trinidad are translated (concretized) into three essential elements: steelpan, calypso and masquerade. As Richard Schechner explains »there are historical- traditional rather that logical-performance reasons why mas (masquerade), new characters and traditional characters, various official competitions, calypso, pan, and kalinda are all performed at carnival.«[163]

One of the musical codes of Carnival is characterized by a »sweet beat« of the steel pan, whose unmistakable melody accompanies the principal festival events. The percussion instrument made of 55 gallon oil drum evolved out of earlier musical practices of enslaved African and Afro-descendants.

---

161 Burton, Richard, E.D (1997): »Afro- Creole, Power, Opposition, and Play in the Caribbean«, Cornell University Press, Ithaca and London, p. 156
162 Mason, Peter (1998): »Bacchanal! The Carnival Culture in Trinidad«, Temple University Press, Philadelphia, pp. 7-16
163 Schechner, Richard: »Carnival (Theory) After Bakhtin«, in Riggio (2004): op. cit,p.6

The African populations used skin drums for communication, religious ceremonies, and as an element which went along the dances and the *chantewell* songs as interlude to the *stickfights*. The late years of the 19th centuries were characterized by events which led to an irreversible change and innovation in the concept of playing the drum. In fact, in the 1883 the use of drums in street parades was outlawed, as the British feared that the passing of secret messages by means of drumming might become the impetus for social unity and revolt among the Blacks.

Since music is a vital expression of life and culture, and the drums are of great importance both in African and Indian culture- rhythm being one of the most important elements of African and Indian based music, and thereby a fundamental part of their worship, when the skin drums were banned, its rhythm and functions were replaced by sticks, especially with bamboo sticks which could be tuned into an instrument consequentially called *Tamboo Bamboo* (Blake 1995). Because of their »second« use as weapons against other bands and the police, which brought to their banning in the 1930s, and the serious injuries inflicted on the foot of the player by the repeated pounding on the ground, a gradual change to street instruments in street bands began to take place. The year of 1938 is considered as the birth of the steel drum when *Tamboo Bamboo* bands were finally switching over to steel.

The first true *steelpan* used by musicians was an empty biscuit container, and it was just a matter of time before the act of beating steel could be developed and transformed in a more complex sequence of different tones. In fact, Pan music developed rapidly during the late 1930s, and by 1941 many *steelbands* playing in Trinidad became popular among U.S. soldiers based on the naval bases on the island. On one hand, this process was facilitated by the banning of playing during the war years, which gave people more time for acoustic experimentation with the emerging steel drum; on the other, the oil industry and the US naval base with their abundance of oil drums, which were successively cut and used as dustbins, replaced the biscuit tins as the raw material for pan making.

Originally associated with criminals, the lower class and the street clashes among rival groups, after the Second World War the steel pan music gradually gained respectability and fame.

By the end of the 50s, the steel pan was so popular that it was chosen as a part of the Commonwealth celebration held in London. As a result, since those years the *steelpan* has been strongly identified as an important element of Trinidadian pride, and became one of the symbols of the national culture.

The musical counterpart of the steel pan is Calypso. According to Peter Mason »Calypso lives and breathes carnival«[164], for it represents the oratory of the Caribbean expressed as a musical performance. Its rhythms can be traced back to the African slaves' arrivals in the New World, which during the course of history combined with some elements of the European music tradition, such, for instance, the ballade. The word calypso probably comes from the Hausa »*Kaiso*«, a praise/critical singer from West Africa (Carol 1998), which is still largely used, especially by many *calypsonians*.

As Gordon Rohdher asserted: »the history of Calypso is that of urbanization, immigration and black reconstruction in post-emancipation Trinidad...one possible approach to writing a history of the calypso in Trinidad would be to identify its west African roots and then to trace what happened to that oral tradition in colonial Trinidad, where there was a phenomenal mixture of peoples, languages and customs.«[165]. Indeed this African rooted particular form of folk song, which historically conditioned by its new environment, developed distinctively in Trinidad into a form of people's art, whose lyrics, melody and performances are uniquely Caribbean.

Modern calypso is related to the world of the *chantewells*, who were the lead singers of the *canboulay* or *kalinda* bands. In the past the *chantewells* were mostly performed by women, who sang and danced as an interlude in *stickfighting* yards. It was a call and response song, which after the post emancipation period gradually evolved in song duels, called *picong*, staged in calypso tents where there were performed confrontations between *calypsonians*, who, although being still linked with a band, by the end of the 1930s concentrated on competing for cash prizes. The texts started to be written in English, and were

---

164 Mason: op. cit., p.9
165 Rohlehr, Gordon (1990): »Calypso and Society in Pre- Independence Trinidad«, Lexicon Trinidad Ltd, , Port of Spain, p. 1

characterized by spicy commentaries on the political and social scandals, obscenities, and jokes. *Calypsonian* is the man of the word, who, according to the African tradition of the utility of the music whose purpose is for social control, with his performance articulating and symbolizing the thoughts and values of a particular audience, by sharing, defining and criticizing issues belonging to that world of which they are equally part.

The basic structural unit of the festival is the masquerade, or *mas*, as it is known in Trinidad. Every year thousands of people, Trinidadians and visitors, erupt on the road, wining (a typical Caribbean dance, consisting in rotating the hips and waist), and chipping (the way of putting one foot after the other) following the rhythm of the last *Soca* (a kind of »calypso's son« developed in interaction with the African-American music, whose gestator was Lord Shorty in the early 70s) hits played loudly by big trucks, with no interruption for one night (playing *jouvert*, event which opens the Carnival) and two days (Carnival Monday and Tuesday or Mardi Gras) throughout Port of Spain.

Costume bands parade the streets depicting modern, and ancient history and creative art. In fact each band portrays a theme which may be drawn from history, literature, folklore, fantasy, current events, or virtually any domain of popular culture. The kinds of masks played in the last hundreds years of Carnival are extremely varied, for they underwent diverse changes throughout the island's socio-political and economic history[166], that led carnival to the shape it has in this century.

Before the »bikini« bands, which now outnumber on the streets on Carnival Tuesday, before the theatrical epics of Peter Minshall, who brought new dynamism to the masquerade combining tradition and innovation, before the fantasy representations of Wayne Berkeley and before the historical epics of George Bailey (to name just a few of the most famous Mas designers), on the street there were *Poirrot Granade*, often with a book in his hand wearing a dress made of coloured strips; the

---

[166] For instance the participation of the middle class in the 19th century, and the oil boom in the '70s, whose consequences of wealth increase through the population, led to a changing in the aesthetic of carnival and in the experimentation of new materials (Green/ Scher 2007: 5)

Midnight Robber, with his wide hat and his »robber talk« aimed to scare the audience and taking some money from them; the *Dame Lorraine*, played always by a man and grossly misrepresenting French planters' wives; the *Baby Doll*, with their white faces and their babies in their arms in the search of economic support from the absent father; the *Jab-Jab, Jab Molassis, Moko Jumbies*, dancing on stilts echoing typical African masquerade; *Blue* and *Red Devils*, that populate covered in mud the *Jouvay* (*Jouvert*) bands, the dragons, the *Bookman*, with his book filled with names of dead people designated to the hell; the *white and black faced Minstrels*; the *fancy* and *bad behaviour Sailors*; the *fancy Indians* and the *Spanish Burriquitos*.

Fig.1: Moko Jumbies

Sunshine Snacks Junior Carnival 2006, Downtown Port of Spain, Trinidad &Tobago

Fig.2: Bookman

Demonstration of traditional characters at the Centre for Creative and Festival Arts, St. Augustine Campus, UWI, Trinidad & Tobago

Fig.3: Blue Devils

Blue Devils Competition 2006, Paramin, Trinidad&Tobago

Fig.4: Blue Devils

Fig.5: Dame Lorraine

Mas in Victoria Square 2006, Port of Spain, Trinidad & Tobago

Fig.6: Baby Doll

Fig.7: Minstrels

Mas in Victoria Square 2006, Port of Spain, Trinidad & Tobago

Fig.8: Burrokeet (Burroquite)

Sunshine Snacks Junior Carnival 2006, Downtown Port of Spain, Trinidad &Tobago

Fig.9: Moko Jumbies

Parade of Bands 2006, Streets of Port of Spain, Trinidad & Tobago

Fig.10: Fancy Indians

Parade of Bands 2006, Streets of Port of Spain, Trinidad & Tobago

These masquerades, which are the result of the encounters of different traditions and folklore, mainly African and European, are nowadays portrayed on the street principally on the Friday before Ash Wednesday during the traditional carnival characters' festival.

In Trinidad, *Mas* is the visual attraction *par excellence*: it is art, profit, parody, and, *in primis*, the theatrical persona that desires to reaffirm its identity via performance. Earl Lovelace accurately describes through Aldrick, the protagonist of his famous novel »The Dragon Can't Dance«, the meaning hidden behind a carnival mask and the act of wearing it:

»[...] the making of his dragon costume was to him always a new miracle, a new test not only of its skill but of his faith: for though he knew exactly what he had to do, it was only by faith that he could bring alive from these scraps of cloth and tin that dragon, its mouths breathing fire, its tail trashing the ground, its nine chains rattling, that would contain the beauty and threat and terror that was the message he took every year to Port of Spain. It was in this message that he asserted before the world his self. It was through it that he demanded that others see him, recognize his personhood, be warned of his dangerousness.«[167]

Thus masks are not merely pictures of other beings, but might be fundamentally the way in which the identity of those beings is attributed to or predicated by the mask wearer as well. On this regard Milla Cozart Riggio pointed out that: »[...] Trinidad and Tobago Carnival celebrates the beauty of the masquerarder and affirms an identity which is always present (if submerged) in the island, rather than inverting an existing hierarchical structure«[168] Indeed, Carnival is more than a display of parading floats and maskers; it is, in fact, the imaginative medium, the body of codes and conventions, of signs and signals, by which Trinidadians affirm their individuality within the society.

In Trinidad Carnival »play mas« are two elements intrinsically interwoven. The act of playing has much more in common

---

167 Lovelace, Earl (1998): »The Dragon Can't Dance«, Faber and Faber Limited, London, pp. 27-28.
168 Riggio (1998): op. cit., p. 15

with the Yoruba performances, rather than with the European use of the word. Margaret Thompson Drewal explains that:

»Performing ritual is at once 'hard work' and 'playing'. What play is not for Yoruba is unserious, frivolous and impotent.«[169]

The personality, the experiences and the very nature of the mask wearer's reaction change, and he will be no longer identified with the previous person, but with the character he is playing; if he is a dancer, the whole style of his dance will be dictated by mask, that is, the Latin persona, a being without life till he adopts it, which comes from without seizes upon him and proceeds to substitute itself into him. Thus, the praise-songs, call and response, improvisational jam, drumming rhythms, dances, imply a particular kind of production of meaning and a particular cultural creation.

During the last decades carnival also became the synonym of Caribbean culture and a symbol of pride, which had to be organized, and therefore controlled, by the supervision of the National Carnival Commission. The festival performances were consequentially channelled into various events: the steel pan competitions with their apex in the Panorama Final, the calypso tents with their Claypso Monarch, Soca Monarch prize, the King and Queen competitions for the masquerade, and finally on carnival Tuesday the election of the band of the year and the road march of the year, that is, the calypso melody most heard to the accompaniment of the bands in the procession. Indeed, in Trinidad, the seriousness of playing (which also characterises the various competitions) is *dis-played* on the streets, offering simple and visual pleasure, which echoes the goliardic freedom and topsy-turvy world of the European carnival tradition with its idea of a collective release of energy and inhibitions.

The hybrid nature of carnival reveals that the underlying features of the festival are intrinsic to the dialectics of social classifications and social relations within the Caribbean society both in a local and global context. The dynamic of Carnival is regulated by the mutual relation of these two forces, which reflect the dichotomy of values that govern the internal structure

---

169   Drewal, Thompson, Margaret: op. cit., p. 15

of the society. Caribbean society, in fact, is still characterized by foundational opposites (for instance high/low, black/white, inside/outside, male/female etc) which, on their turn, are inseparable from the dialectic of »respectability« -the super structure, the outside, the colonial legacy- and »reputation«- internally generated value system opposed to the externally generated system of respectability- (Wilson 1973). These two elements are translated into two versions of carnival: the Dionysian that is seen as the total freedom, and the Appolinean that tries to deviate from the Dionysian in the search for a better harmony.

Carnival by exaggerating, inverting, re-forming, magnifying, minimizing, *dis-colouring* and re-colouring social aspects and chronicled events, for its intrinsic capacity of being reflexive, arouses »consciousness of ourselves as we see ourselves«.[170] In fact, Peter Stalybrass and Alone White, by explaining the social mechanisms of carnival and masquerading, asserted that: »The carnivalesque mediates between a classical/classificatory body and its mediation, its Others, what it excludes to create its identity as such«.[171]

Carnival in Transition: Unmasking on the Street, Masking on the Stage. Dynamics and Contradictions of Women's Participation in Carnival

> »Este fenómeno de las mujeres en la Revolucíon es una Revolución dentro de otra Revólucion.«*
> (Fidel Castro)

Trinidad Carnival is undergoing a social, gender, economical and political metamorphosis. This century is the time when

---

170 Myerhoff, Barbara (1980): »Life History among the Elderly: Performance, Visibility, and Remembering«, Kurt, Beck (edited by) (1986): »Studies of the Human Life Course, American association for the Advancement of Studies«, in Turner (1986): op. cit, p. 42
171 Stallybrass/White: op. cit., p. 26
* My translation: »This phenomenon of the women in the Revolution is a Revolution within another Revolution.«

women are proclaiming their sovereignty, by erupting on the street, wining in their small and colourful costumes, becoming one of the most disputed attractions of the festival itself. In fact, since the middle 80s, the participation of women of all classes and colour in Trinidad carnival precipitated an astonishing rise, making their presence more predominant than ever, and, by so doing, challenging carnival's aesthetic panorama and deepest contests.

At first sight, the memory goes back to the *pissenlit* of the nineteenth century, when women were also central to the construction of this *jamettes* carnival (Brereton 1975) and thereby caused as much as a stir in their time as does wining today. Although it is commonplace that carnival enacts an inversion of the ordinary world by objectifying some other possibilities, this event may be interpreted in relation to certain recent shifts in the wider context of sexuality, gender relations and economical factors as a consequence of the changes caused by the cultural clash of colonial and postcolonial society.

In Trinidad, entertainment has incorporated aspects of the sacred and ceremonial dances by making them into voices of social protest and cultural renewal, instilling in the people a renewed sense of cultural pride and solidifying the values of the community. The melancholic man with his vestiges of dragons and *jab jab*, the scholars and old fashioned carnival appassionato who crowd the street downtown at the *ole' mas* parade, worry about the vulgarity and lasciviousness of the new fashion *pretty mas*, and concern about an imminent loss of the precious and global famous Caribbean stigma. The contemporary carnival parade has been accused of public display of obscenity, of meaningless and aesthetic/creative less costumes and of inauthenticy, since they are seen as the antithesis of what Errol Hill describes as the principles of Trinidad Carnival that are mandate of the National Theatre, »will truly represent the cultural attitudes, expressions and aspirations of the people of Trinidad and Tobago«, by having achieved »a synthesis between old and new, between folk forms and art forms, between native and alien traditions«[172].

---

172 Hill (1997): op. cit., p. 115

Carnival's emphasis on the mode of excess and reversal has always undermined the categories of social privilege, displaying a certain uniformity of identity within the process of masquerading and embodying an ongoing struggle against inequality and oppression. These ritualized forms of conflict, both physical and verbal, became an important part of the post-emancipation carnival. Indeed, according to Patricia de Freitas, »Carnival was considered uniquely Trinidadian, the womb which gave birth to steel band music and calypso, two inventions of the black, urban, lower class males«[173]. In fact, since the national *mythopoesis* is profoundly gendered, »Like most nationalists, the architects of Trinidad's nationhood were men who assumed the premise of an identity discourse which pitted the indigenous Self against the elite and/or foreign Other. The logic of this discourse reduced all oppositions within the carnival into 'resistance', against dominant elites, privileging the behaviour typically associated with male resistance practices.«[174]

In the early 20th century Carnival is created within a fundamentally male space, where its characters were enveloped within a cultural nationalist discourse providing iconic representations of the black masculinity which had to be regenerated at all costs. In the newly independent nation black men had to be reconstituted as protagonist without being constantly confronted with the dilemma »turn with or disappear«[175]; therefore Carnival became the place where men negotiate masculine honour and reputation, where »Fisheye at least found a place [the steel pan band] where he could be a man, where its strength and quickness had meaning and he could feel pride in belonging and purpose to his living, and where he had all the battles he had dreamed of, and more, to fight«[176]. The reproductive modalities of self affirmation were, indeed, inextricabily linked with the myth of maleness and nationhood, and conse-

---

[173] De Freitas, Patricia, A. (1999): »Disrupting the Nation: Gender and Transformations in the Trinidad Carnival«, New West Indian Guide/Nieuwe West-Indische Gids, 73 1 et 2, KITLV, Leiden, the Netherlands, p. 11
[174] Ibid, p. 13
[175] Fanon (1986): op. cit, p. 100
[176] Lovelace: op. cit., p. 68

quently constructed on the dichotomies such as reputation/respectability, hard/sweet, male/female.

Caribbean society has commonly been characterized by a cultural dualism abstractly conceived as a structure of opposition that Wilson calls »reputation« and »respectability«. For Wilson, men's worlds are imbued with the ethos of »*reputation*«, an egalitarian value system of local origin which emphasizes virility, sexual conquests and public swearing and fighting. »Respectability«, by contrast, is rooted in social and class stratification and colonially-derived notions of status and comportment, through which women are associated with the domestic and interiorising modes which would trap them into a facade of marriage and responsibility (Wilson 1973). Thus, according to Wilson:

»In their relation to each other and to their environment people classify themselves on the basis of their differences. The environment is, in a sense, appropriate to signify these differences, and at this level of conceptualization we can identify a social structure of a mechanistic nature founded on social class. But this stratification depends on and is the result of what people think to be significant as difference. They have in mind a philosophical principle or 'policy', as Hulme calls it, from which they can instil, defend and justify their actions. The principle of stratification that subsumes all other in the Caribbean is, I suggest, the principle of respectability. [...] There is, however a particular level of structure which is the dialectical complement of stratification and respectability and which support an idea of social equality. At the empirical, mechanical level of structure this is to be found in the interpretation of kinship ties on the one hand and in the elaboration and specification of friendship ties on the other. These latter are centred in groups called crews. The philosophical principle by which equality is guided, which 'man have in mind', is what I have designated reputation. [...] Thus reputation is largely specific to men, while respectability is most particular to women and concerns only men at certain times of their lives, or only in certain men in the society. [...] Respectability has its roots in the external colonizing (or quasi-colonizing) society, though in any given instance its reality depends on the integral role of the colonizing society in the social system of the colony. Reputation, on the other hand, is 'indigenous' to the colony (or quasi-colony) and is both an authentic structural principle and a counterprinciple.«[177]

In the West Indies, men and women have been deeply socialized into certain sex-roles and attitudes, for gender categories are social constructions with a cultural specificity, and thereby sustained by a system of symbols, meanings, ascriptions and expectations. Indeed, the Caribbean male's quest (that is, the quest of the warriors who fight for independence) of valorising his masculinity and becoming visible found its expression on Carnival's symbolic battle ground.

Since carnival is the site around which different social identities are defined and confirmed, in Trinidad »*playing mas*« signify something besides the basic visual and performative fact of a person in a costume dancing and misbehaving on the street, becoming the *mythopoesis* of the new nation. Thus, as Patricia de Freitas pointed out, »Yet paradoxically, the narrative of nationalism is largely about men giving birth to the nation through struggle and the 'hard' values of 'resistance'. Carnival as the symbolic site of the struggle has largely been conceptualized as male. As a privileged site of male oppositional and reputation male-practicing, Carnival is narrated as the male 'womb' in which the real Self was nurtured and from which the 'nation' was born.«[178] On the contrary, women had to »fit« in the master narrative as the passive representers of the respectable culture.

In public discourses a split image of women and an ambivalent attitude toward them, that must be dealt with the carnival emerge. There is, in fact, a tendency to split women, symbolically in two opposite characters, that is the pure and the defiled, that achieve its clearest expression in the texts of the calypsonians. The image of women is distorted in the overlay of the male singer's ideology, by reinforcing through dual textual and semantic orientation the masculine/master order which invites

---

[177] Wilson, J., Peter (1995): »Crab Antics, A Caribbean Case Study of the Conflict Between Reputation and Respectability«, Waveland Press, United States of America, pp. 8-9
[178] De Freitas (1999): op. cit., p. 14

woman- the sexual object- to participate in a ludic dialogue that ensures »natural« compliance with male dominance.

The image of woman is, on the one hand, idealized as Mother, the house/inside nourisher and provider, and on the other repudiated as the shameless whore, the one who ventured out in the public men's domain (Rohlehr 1990:223-24), that is the *jamette*, the prostitute, the subaltern »Other« beyond the boundaries of the acceptable society. Carnival, and above all calypso, has always mirrored gender relation and the public display of sexuality which pervade all aspects of life in the Caribbean. For instance, Yevilgton explains that:

»Sexuality, gender relations and flirting are related to particular Caribbean kinship arrangements whereby male-female relationships are thought of in terms of exchange. Sexuality becomes a transfer point of money and power and a locus of control. [...] Flirting is part of a process in which younger women are eventually made to be 'respectable' as they grow older, in order to fend off sexual advances of men. Flirting, with violent overtones, is responsible for enforcing respectability, which is both subordination to hegemonic values of passivity and piety and liberation from direct sexual harassment.[...] At the same time, rather than directly upholding the values of authority, this may very well be the most effective way to resist authority. Women's flirting and 'heckling', on the other hand, are behaviours in which women attempt to mitigate and resist men's control. In many ways, women's initiation of flirting ensures some measure of control over the situation. [...] These power relations themselves are not given but constructed in pitched battles to decide meaning and interpretation. These battles are won and lost and the victor gets to determine the terms of the armistice, at least temporarily, when systems of meaning are created and enforced by groups with the most power.«[179]

Thus, the social and political structure that surrounds the festival is the agent that determines perceptions of what the event is about and should concern. Therefore, the unruly woman of the last two decades of Carnival might not just be pictured as an expression of sexuality with no object but itself, and as the en-

---

179 Yelvington, Kevin, A (1996): »Flirting in the factory«, Journal of the Royal Anthropological Institute, Vol. 2, pp. 330-31

actment of an absolute freedom rather than an inversion of cultural values, but as rehearsal perfomative act, that may be understood within a dramaturgy of power first exhibiting what it consigns the oblivion. Moreover, rather than the *jammettes*, who might be the typical representation of the medieval grotesque body described by Bakhtin, the unmasked woman may echo in the Maenads' ritual in homage to Dionysus, or the West African cults of spirit possession, which both attract more women than men, suggesting that ritual experience serves to free it from limitations of prior association, to pose challenging problems, and to encourage reflection on the everyday life.

The canalising functions of obscenity and abuse can be contextualised in relation to homage and praise, and locally historicised in the social memory of sexual politics. For instance, within the Yoruba populations, performers use the structure of ritual to reflect on gender and sex role division. In her analysis of Yoruba ritual, Margaret Thompson Drewal asserts that:

»For the most part Yoruba art depicts ritual roles of men and women so that there is a thematic consistency between the two forms of representation. Each drives meaning in relation to the other in time and space. The dominant themes of maleness depicted in sculpture are hunter/ warrior, herbalist/diviner, drummer, king, bush animal, and woman's partner. In contrast, females are typically shown as mother, priestess, bird, and men's partner. The depiction of motherhood has ritual significance even though it is not often a ritual role per se ...Whereas it is primarily women who nurture the gods, men in Yoruba society mask. Yoruba construct performance roles like they construct gender, that is based on the anatomical and biological features involved specifically in procreation. [...] In masking, men cover and conceal their exteriors. But when women are 'mounted' by a deity in possession trance, the spirit of that deity enters her 'inner head', her interior. Men, in becoming procession priests, are therefore like women in relationship to the deity; they are receptacles. Crossing gender boundaries, male priests cross dress as woman, and priestesses possessed by male deities select out forceful, direct dynamic movement qualities ordinarily associated with men. [...] At the basis taboo against women wearing a mask may be a tacit understanding of what Christopher Crocker (1997:59) call the contagious power of metonymic conjunction. That is there is an analogical relationship between a pregnant woman and a full body mask. The metonymic conjunction may explain the prevalence of African myths that attribute the very origin of masking to women (Cole 1985:15). *Metaphorically speaking, woman was the original mask*.*«[180]

Similarly, in ancient Greece, during the Dionysian festivities, the tension between women's lived bodily experiences, and the cultural meanings inscribed on the female body used to be translated through the socio-cultural contexts of fertility, witchcraft and madness. In fact, as Eva C. Keuls points out:

»One of the epithets of the god Dionysus was 'he who drives women mad' (gynaimanes), and this title points to the curious circumstance that, in the Dionysiac rituals, only the woman go crazy, while the men merely act out a part. The Maenads, in their most unrestrained behaviour, act like a person in an aesthetic trance: they throw back their heads, raise their arms in wild gestures; and maul animals, mostly young ones, in the cruellest fashion, and brandish their severed limbs. They let snakes entwine their arms, and they ululate and make a noise with clappers and tympana. [...] The background is filled with Dionysus' vines. In the encounter with Maenads, the satyrs' function is mainly to molest, but not to rape, their female companions, and in turn to suffer violence from the women, who attack them in self defence. [...] The men are masked and decked out in satyr garb, but the women are not in any way identified as Maenads.«[181]

Apparently these ritual practices have persisted, transformed and been translated in the contemporary Caribbean carnival, cast in performances in a myriad of ways, as parade, masking display, dances and musical performances, evoking the reflexive, progressive, transformative experience of ritual participation.

In the West Indian society -where a number of cultural and socio-historical influences, dating back to the experience of slavery and Emancipation, are held in a contradictory and

---

*   My Italics
180   Drewal, Thompson, Margaret: op. cit., pp. 174-75, 184-85
181   Keuls, Eva, C. (1993): »The Reign of the Phallus, Sexual Politics in Ancient Athens«, University of California Press, London, pp. 360-62

transgressive tandem- gender relations and women status inhered and reflect the enormous complication arising from the basic mismatch between the women's reality and the official dogmas, systematically entrenched through formal education.

Thus, according to Curdella Forbes, »On the one hand, gender experiences were deeply inflected by socio-economical realities that constantly shifted the authorities associated with masculinity between male and female members of society. As a direct result of this, West Indian society has been variously described as 'matrifocal' and 'matriarchal'. [...] On the other hand, vestiges of the colonial education system in the form of ideas of the female as breadwinner, household ruler, public authority and social pioneer were valorized.«[182]

Caribbean woman embodied the inheritance of both the economically independent West African Women and of the »upper class Maenads« (who normally used to live segregated in the husband's house), and, like them, she uses the »Caribbean National Ritual« par excellence to display this contradictory ambivalence. In fact, Pamela R. Franco, paraphrasing John Berger in the »Way of Seeing«, asserts that:

»women's dress and dressing up allow them to become both object and subject, or what he terms 'the surveyed' and the 'surveyor'. As objects of the male gaze, women are the surveyed. However, in the act of 'watching' themselves, a ritual that is learned at a young age, women become surveyors. Berger, here, introduces the idea of women as subjects or agents (surveyors) capable of constructing and manipulating their self-image. Revisionist scholars, expanding on the concept of women as subjects, emphasize the ways in which women manipulate dress and dressing up- particularly as a strategy to attain visibility and to articulate particular concerns, be they cultural, economical, personal or political. [...] The body of literature positions women as agents with clearly defined intentions, which they express or communicate through dress and dressing up. Agency here is neither fixed nor permanent; it is negotiated at particular historical moments or on specific occasions. Carnival is one

---

182 Forbes, Curdella (2005): »From nation to Diaspora, Samuel Selvon, George Lamming and the Cultural Performance of Gender«, The University of West Indies Press, Mona Kingston, Jamaica p. 29

such occasion when woman use dress and dressing up to create a self image through which they can 'articulate' their opinion.«[183]

In Trinidad Carnival this process is translated in an alternating »dressing up« and »dressing down«, depending on the circumstances in which femininity and the female body is »acting out«. Thus the increasing phenomenon of women as subject/object of carnival is part of a broader power relations determined by local factors and international forces, which lead to different and often contradictory interpretations.

On one hand, according to some scholars like Richard Burton, the women's exploit might be read as the consequence of their economic and social improvement; in fact, in his study on the Afro-Caribbean culture, he asserts: »Perhaps a social revolution as profound as that of emancipation was beginning to manifest itself in carnival and elsewhere as Trinidadian women, pushed to the margins of carnival after 1884, apparently regained, more or less exactly a century later, the central position of their infamous and illustrious forebears: Boadicea, Myrtle the Turtle, and Long Body Ada.«[184]

Philip W. Scher and Garth L. Green point out that the oil boom of the 70s and the consequent increase in personal and public wealth had a positive influence on the number of middle class people participating in Carnival, and consequently on the changing of the carnival aesthetic, for they were willing to spend and invest more money on the Carnival, transforming the festival according to the middle class values. The subsequent oil bust and the »industrialization by invitation« oriented on the export required cheap labour, which means, in the developing countries, women's labour (Barriteau 1998:202), led to a significant economical independence for women (although in the Caribbean it is not synonymous with empowerment), which consequently was reflected in their increasing participation in Carnival.

---

183 Franco, R., Pamela: »The Martinican, dress and politics in nineteenth-century Trinidad Carnival«, in Riggio (2004): op. cit., p.64
184 Burton: op. cit, p. 209

A third determined feature was the transformation of the Carnival complex from vulgar, lower class festival into the symbol of the independent Trinidad and Tobago, that is, the Trinbagonian national pride. The interaction of these factors led gradually to the present day female sovereignty in carnival. For instance, Sammy Espinet, a member of the first and most famous female steel band orchestra »The Girls Pat« (1952), told me in an interview, that they were not allowed to play on the street, for in the early 50s the steel pan bands were still associated with poverty and violence. Although the ideological impediment, they resounded a great success, which culminated with the invitation to play at the First minister house, in Jamaica and in Guyana, preparing the ground for their female descendants, who today play in a great number of steel pan orchestras.

Unfortunately, these remarks are just a partial interpretation of a complex and multifaceted phenomenon, or better said, it is just one side of the coin, since, especially in the Caribbean, »economical independence« and »expanded educational opportunities« are not synonymous for »empowerment«. In fact, even though the great participation of women in carnival may be a sign of their economic and pedagogical improved conditions (for example, in the case of the steel pan, which is taught in schools), the display of women's assertion is attenuated by the fact that female appropriation of male coded forms of sexual objectification might be conservative rather than libratory.

Fig. 11: Women and the Pan

Bands Parade, Carnival Tuesday 2006, Streets of Port of Spain, Trinidad & Tobago

The ambivalence between women's life experiences and the ideologies in which they are trapped is translated in the carnevalesque women's subversion and appropriation of male-identified forms of sexual display that may actually serve to reinforce the patriarchal structures that it otherwise criticizes. On this regard, Gordon Rohelehr observed that: »Soca songs recognize the wild winer woman and appeal to her through a series of slogan-commands in which she is instructed to wine, grind, jump-up, jump-down ... with various aspects of her anatomy ... [W]omen [are] herd[ed] into a collective space where under the illusion of empowerment they move to the shouted commands of the soca men. And just as soca invites women to unmask their sexuality, it also represents the male as predator and voyeur.«[185]. Furthermore the sexual oriented tour-

---

*   Place for pre carnival preparation (costume designing and making)

185 Rohlehr, Gordon (1998): » 'We Getting the Kaiso That We Deserve': Calypso and the World Music Market«, Drama Revue 42, no. 3 Fall 1998, pp. 89-90.

ism industry and the carnival local/ international oriented business, aliment the already complex contradiction that inhabits the festival. In the past two decades Carnival has been guided more firmly by market forces than by creative ambition, becoming the most lucrative business of the region.

According to Lévy Strauss women circulate as signs, but they are not theorized as sign producers (Russo 1995:328), which means that, in the carnival business the object/woman becomes a very lucrative sign. The industrialization by invitation based on cheap women labour seems to have been translated in the tight/creative and fabric/less bikini costumes worn mostly by women.

The past production of the *mas camp** based on the creativity, uniqueness and success of the designer, and on the collaboration of the yard people, who used to volunteer in the *mas camp*, spending days and sleepless nights sewing costumes, has been replaced by bikini costumes mass productions, which, despite the poverty of the manufacture they do not compare with the selling price of the costume itself, are very required both for the local and »inter-islands« carnival markets.

For instance, I remember that, when I was sent to the mundane Country Club to see the selling process of the costumes designed by Island People (a new and trendy young band that might challenge Poison's podium), I was surprised to see the amount of costumes of different bands, the different organizations and people, since I was expecting to see something similar to Peter Minshall's mas camp: the »Calaloo Company«.

A woman from the staff explained to me that the location was the selling point for several costumes of different bands, which usually use the mas camp to design the costumes models which are then sent somewhere else for the realization (sewing etc.), and finally left in the »hands« of a company (where actually that woman was employed) responsible for the selling process of the costumes for both carnival in Trinidad and diverse festivals in other islands of the Archipelago. Indeed, according to Peter Mason, »Trinidad's way of life is now constantly buffeted by commercialism as well as the modern obsession with size and superficial beauty. Carnival has increasingly come to reflect these global obsessions.«[186]

Fig.12: Queen's head (mas in the making)

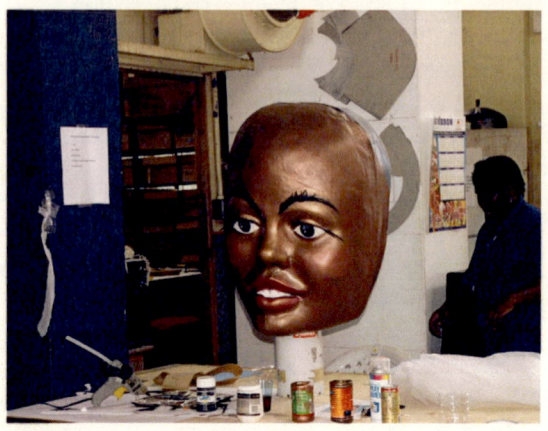

Fig. 13: Working at the mas camp

Callaloo Company, Peter Minshall, Chaguaramas, Port of Spain, Trinidad & Tobago, 2006

---

186   Mason: op. cit.,p.159

Fig.14: Selling point, Island People's costumes

Fig. 15: Selling point, Island's People costumes

Country Club, Maraval, Port of Spain, Trinidad & Tobago

Camera lenses, controlled mostly by men, continually zoom in on the women in the band, cable television networks make images of Carnival revellers available to global audiences, sponsoring Trinidad as an island of exotic women and cavorting female bodies, alimenting the stereotype of an unruly and promiscuous place.

Caribbean islands are increasingly incorporating sexuality into their national strategies for competing in the globalized economy, embedding this sexual market in industries that are tightly integrated into the global economy, such as tourism and mining. Thus, in the name of a global capitalism, the artists have to accommodate their creativity for the anonymity implied by the mass production, and the women's carnival participation in the name of emancipation and resistance has been shadowed by the collusion of global capitalism in the marketing and commodification of Caribbean popular culture.

Fig16.: Island People

Parade of Bands, Carnival Tuesday 2006, Streets of Port of Spain, Trinidad & Tobago

Fig.17: Poison

Fig. 18: Island People

Parade of Bands, Carnival Tuesday 2006, Streets of Port of Spain, Trinidad & Tobago

Victor Turner, quoting Sign's theory about cultural performances as cultural media which, combined in various ways are able to express and communicate the contents of a given culture, asserted: »rituals, drama, and other performative genres, are often orchestrations of media, not expression in a single medium«[187].

The validity of Carnival, which is a high performative genre, depends on its capacity of absorbing and expressing the present by containing the past. Thus, the contemporary carnival is neither a sign of decline nor a rupture with the old, but the dynamic »magical mirror« (Turner 1986) of the Trinidadians, which is rooted in the social reality and not imposed upon it. Moreover, »cultural performances are not simple reflectors or expressions of culture or even of changing culture, but many themselves been active agencies of change, representing the eye by which culture sees itself and the drawing board on which creative actors sketch out what they believe to be more apt or interesting 'designs for living'«[188].

Not only is carnival, as part of the ideological production, generated out of conflict and contradiction, but it also addresses women, and to some extent men, on the issue of the contradiction that govern women's lives. In fact, Natalie Zemon Davis, in her study on society and culture in early modern France, points out that:

»Play with the unruly woman is partly a chance for temporary release from the traditional and stable hierarchy; but it is also part of the conflict over efforts to change the basic distribution of power within the society. The women on top might even facilitate innovation in historical theory and political behaviour.«[189]

The mutual and dialectical relationship between structure and anti structure, that is, between society and carnival, not only allows the predominant presence of women in the contemporary

---

187 Turner (1986): op. cit., p. 23
188 Ibid, p. 24
189 Davis Zemon Natalie (1975): »Society and Culture in early modern France«, Gerald Duckworth Company Limited. London, p. 132

Trinidad carnival, but also the possibility for them to challenge the structure's ideological assumptions, altering the social structure as it is presently constituted. By introducing antistructural values into it, which consequently may lead to the formation of new spaces in a man's world. Indeed, as the historical, political and economic changes that challenge the societal structure are further reflected and performed in the antistructure of carnival, so the shifts that effect the antistructure may have repercussions on the structure's societal, economical and political domains, for both structure and anti structure stand in a mutual and continuous relationship to each other.

Throughout the years, the various local and global circumstances that challenged the respectability/normative structure, made possible the women's participation in the ritual/carnival process as subject rather than marginal elements of the festival context (prostitutes, street vendors, tailors). The reputation sphere which has been always associated with masculinity and violence has started to be penetrated and changed by the increasing presence of women in all carnival disciplines.

Calypso is considered the least conducive element to the participation of women, and it is the place par excellence which has been mostly associated with what Rohlehr calls »a predominately male mode, whose themes are manhood and the identity of the individual within the group«[190]. Even though both Pearse and Hill revealed the presence of women as *chantewell* (Pearse 1988:58) or as *cariso*'s performers (Hill 1997: 58), by the turn of the twentieth century they disappeared from the calypso scene, re-emerging only during the 80s, when a gradual increase of women began to appear on the tents' cast lists.

Although the long held attitudes portraying women as not being able to make good calypsonians are still echoed in diverse polemics on the male song composers' authority upon female calypso texts, female calypsonians continue to grow in stature and prizes. Singing Sandra, for instance, is one of the most famous and successful calypsonians, winning the prestigious title of calypso monarch twice, in 1999 and 2003. She is considered one of the powerful voices of the social conscience, mirrored

---

190 Rohlehr (1990): op. cit., p. 53

not only in the words of her songs, but in her whole persona. Singing Sandra's moralizing stance, which focused on issues of economic injustice and gender inequality and her dominant presence on the stage are not only social oriented critics, but also an enactment of the possibility to challenge the existing unequal gender relations. In fact, as part of the social drama of Trinidad, the success of a calypsonian is also given by his or her capacity of reaching the audience through a performative act, which allows both the performer and the audience to identify themselves with the given issues and vice versa, in a mutual and cathartic social commentary.

In carnival, the visual performative element par excellence is »playing mas«, which is canalized in two different performance practices: playing mas on the road on carnival Monday and Tuesday, and the King and Queen Competitions held at Queen's Park Savannah Stage on the days preceding carnival parades. The »road march« is the most contested carnival event, for it has become, throughout the last twenty years, the female's domain, at least for dancing and wining on the street.

The craft and the art of the mas designers are still largely a male domain and peculiarity. Undoubtedly, at the moment, there is nobody to challenge designers as George Bailey, Wayne Berkeley and Peter Minshall, to name just a few, neither between male nor female designers, but the standardization of the production, based also on an increasing request of younger costumes' designs, led to the employment of new and young talents in diverse mas camps. For instance, Poison, one of the trendiest mas bands between the young generations of Trinidadians, gave the opportunity to young artists like Sandra Hordatt, to gather experience, which is essential for discovering one's own way as an independent mas designer. Sandra Hordatt has become, in fact, a name in the carnival scene, launching in 2006 with four other young mas designers, the competitive band »Island People«.

On one hand, the carnival Queen competition has been always at the centre of debates about the reproduction and commodification of a certain image of Trinidad culture, especially in its early years, when, at the beginning of the 50s, it was instituted under the influence of the American beauty pageants. In fact, like in all beauty contests, where »the idealized femininity put on stage ...is often closely associated with broader concepts such as morality, or larger social entities such as 'the nation'...reinforcing narrow cultural expectations and understandings of women, gender and sexuality.«[191], also in the Trinidad Carnival Queen competitions, the female image promoted on the stage was reflecting the middle-class aspirations of respectability based on western models of beauty. On the other hand, this event could be analysed from another perspective, as Philip Scher points out, assuming that »Respectability and Carnival have been linked since the middle class began to take an active interest in the reformation of the festival, and legacy of competitions, control, and 'improvement' have found their way into Trinidadian life with a variety of consequences«[192]. One of these consequences was that women could enter in much greater number in these purged and respectable-made events, making the first steps to a local and global visibility. In fact, even within a master narrative, carnival has allowed them, and still does, to speak, to challenge the invisibility that has always relied on women throughout the colonial and postcolonial experience.

Women like Alyson Brown, who has been for many years Peter Minshall's Carnival Queen and won twice with him (one in 1990 with the mask »Tan Tan«, -six years later she performed again at the opening ceremony of the Olympic game in Barcelona- and in 1995 with »Joy to the World«) has made her life around the mas, becoming one of the most famous mas women. In an interview, although she did not experience it in first person, (when Peter Minshall asked her to be his Carnival Queen, she was already known in the show business, as a former model and having worked for TV production and theatre), she agreed with the assumption that taking part at the carnival queen competition could open new doors for women, facilitating their self assertion both within the festival context and also in the daily reality. Indeed, whether it is the Carnival Queen

---

191 Cohen, Ballerino, Colleen/ Wilk Richard/ Stoeltje, Beverly (edited by) (1996): Beauty Queens on a Global Stage, Gender, Contests, and Power, , Routledge, New York and London, pp. 3-5

192 Scher, Philip, W. (2003): »Carnival and the Formation of a Caribbean Transnation«, University press of Florida, Gainesville, p. 31

competition, or a Calypso tent, or the road march, or the steel pan Panorama competition, all the various carnival events are: »places where cultural meanings are produced, consumed and rejected, where local and global, ethnic and national, national and international cultures and structures of power are engaged in their most trivial and vital aspects.«[193]

Carnival's metamorphosis is also producing new forms of resistance, for cultural identity and its expressions are more resilient than the local and global forces which might undermine its proliferation. In fact, according to Scher:

»This position holds that whereas foreign products may enter into a local space, where foreign consumer goods may be swamping local versions, there is a transformation that takes place as the 'new' items become reconfigured according to the logic of the local cultural system.«[194]

Referring to the nowadays carnival reality, Scher's assumption means that the new elements, which depended on the festival, at the same time shaped it according to the local cultural systems and values, rather than challenging its forms and meanings. Carnival features, which have been modified in contemporary circumstances by the cultural clash of colonial and postcolonial society, are contextualized, by adapting dynamically to new cultural influences. Indeed, the traditional elements of Carnival do not risk disappearing from the scenes, but they are adapted to the new conditions, by using them for new purposes, without undermining their nature.

Since carnival and comedy are ruled by similar mechanisms, based on the consciously incongruous juxtaposition and exaggeration of the everyday and the extraordinary, traditional carnival characters, by losing their historical contextualized specificity and therefore their comical peculiarity, become consequently symbols of universal values. In fact, for the evolution of the historical facts, from colonization and slavery, to resistance and finally to emancipation and formation of Trinidad and To-

---

193 Cohen/ Wilk/ Stoeltje: op. cit., p. 8
194 Scher, Philip, W. (1999): »Confounding Categories: The Global and the Local in the Process of a Caribbean Art«, Contributors, Small Axe. Vol.: 3. Issue: 6, p. 38

bago are inscribed in the carnival characters of the *book man, dragon, midnight robber, baby doll* etc, these masks become the protagonists of epos of the Trimbagonians' Folk, rather then the topsy-turvy commentary of the market place.

Caribbean carnival is a polysemic event in which each discipline not only entertains, but also constructs cultural memory as a usable past, being, according to Victor Turner, »plural reflexivity« that is, »the ways in which a group or community seeks to portray, understand, and then act on itself«[195]. The code par excellence of the Caribbean reflexivity has always been the syncretic performative mode of carnival. In Trinidad, while the present is reflex and performed on the public stage of carnival, the past is translated and encoded in the traditional characters, which require the Aristotelian temporal and spatial distance of the theatrical stage in order to maintain their reflexivity.

The differences between the topsy-turvy satirical stage of the street and the »tragic« one of theatre, may find a first explanation in Mikhail Bakthin's description of the essential diversity between novel and epic. In fact, according to Bakthin, »the novel comes into contact with the spontaneity of the inclusive present; this is what keeps the genre from congealing«[196] whilst »the world of the epic is the national heroic past ...an absolute epic distance separates the epic world from the contemporary reality, that is, from the time the singer (the author and his audience) lives.«[197]

According to Aristotle epic poetry, comedy and tragedy are all imitation modes of reality (Aristotle, Poetics 12447a), differing from one another in three ways, either by a difference of kind in their means, or by differences in their objects, or in the manner of their imitations. He further asserted that: »Epic poetry, then, has been seen to agree with Tragedy to this extent, that is of being an imitation of serious subjects in a grand kind of verse. It differs from it, however, in its length [...] Tragedy endeavours to keep as far as possible within a single circuit of

---

195 Turner (1979): op. cit., p. 465
196 Bakhtin, Mikhail (1981): »The Dialogic Imagination, Four Essays«, University of Texas Press, Austin,p. 27
197 Ibid, p. 13

the sun...They differ also in their constituents, some being common to both and other peculiar to Tragedy [...] all the parts of an epic are included to Tragedy; but those of Tragedy are not all of them to be found in the Epic«[198] Beside these three formal differences, tragedy differs from the epic poetry for its cathartic feature, which enables the audience to be empathic with the heroes performing on the stage. The object of Tragedy is, in fact, the social thought of a given society, as it was in Athens in V sec BC, with its tensions and contradictions, rising from the new political economical assessments challenging the traditional values on a religious and ethical level.

Tragedy uses, as a source of inspiration for its story and characters, the same elements of the tradition exalted by the epic poets, for exposing them to the public judgment and critic, in the name of the new civic ideal, in front of the metaphorical popular court, represented in the reality by the audience in the theatre. Furthermore the performance is narrated in an »absolute past«, conferring to the drama (the sequences of actions that follow one another in a play) an intelligibility that is not implied in the daily life. That is to say that, the day to day reality is purified from the opacity of the ordinary, which produces in human beings feelings of sorrow, pity and fear, by the *mimesis praxoes*, that is, the dramatic progression of events, which reorganizes summaries and simplifies the human experiences in a mythical past.

On the other hand, in the comedy, the catharsis is not provided by an absolute past and the universalization of the human pains, but articulated by the lens of the laugh, that is, by staging characters portraying the contrary of what the ideal human being is expected to be. Umberto Eco, paraphrasing Pirandello's theory of Humour, explains:

»[...] if the comic is the perception of the opposite, humour is the 'sentiment' of the opposite. A case of comic is a decrepit old woman who smears her face with make-up and dresses like a young girl; facing such

---

198 Aristotle: »Poetics«, in Hofstadter Albert/ Kuhns, Richard (edited by) (1976): »Philosophies of Art and Beauty, Selected Reading in Aesthetics from Plato to Heidegger«, The University of Chicago Press, Chicago, 1449b, 10-15

a picture one notices that this woman is the opposite of what a respectable old woman should be. In a case of humour, one understands why the old woman masks herself, to regain her lost youth.«[199]

By so doing, the human being, who normally undergoes and blames its pains, is able to understand them through the mirror of the drama/laugh mimesis. For its capacity to create and sustain a briefly and intensified social life, the theatre is festive and political as well as literary/ a privileged site for the celebration and critique of the needs and concerns of the polis.

The critical intensification of the collective life represented and experienced on the stage, and the possibilities it creates for action and initiative, make theatre the place where the traditions of collective life that were previously performed in carnival, are objectified and recreated and transformed at their best. The positive critique, by articulating the capacity of popular culture to resist penetration and control by the power culture, inscribed in the traditional characters of carnival, gives rise to dramatic forms that are intensely critical and even experimental in their representation of social and political structure.

In the Caribbean, the re-utilization of traditional characters in theatre also recreate expressive strategies generating a transformative ritual style with a rhythmic spectacle of languages, movements, images and sounds deeply rooted in the social negotiation of church, Carnival and the call-and –response practice of collective experience, which locate the theatrical practices in the continuum of African memory throughout the Diaspora. Thus the Trinidad Carnival, according to Errol Hill, »has in its time encompassed almost every aspect of life and thought of the Trinidad people, and, thus, in content alone, it is a reservoir of material uniquely valuable for a national theatre.«[200]

Between Carnival and theatre there has always been a kind of circularity or, better to say, reciprocal influence, transforming the theatrical into theatre and vice versa. The employment of carnival tropes, like music, calypso, dance, structured around the story, provides a celebration of Caribbean culture and, at the same time a self reflexive critic, creating a sense of unique

---

[199] Eco: op. cit., p. 7
[200] Hill (1997): op. cit., p. 86

Caribbean identity (for instance Derek Walcott's »The Joker of Seville«, Errol Hill's »Man Better Man«, Earl Lovelace's »Jestina Calypso«, or Tony Hall's new attempt to stage Sparrow's famous Calypso song »Jean and Dinah« etc).

Today's carnival, by radically changing the configuration of the festival, led to the formation of new performative spaces for the old carnival characters. They are, in fact, becoming the protagonist of a new *metalanguage* -incorporating both elements of carnival and theatre, both of the indigenous/ African and western tradition- which is canonized in the experimental mode of a new *Commedia dell'Arte*. For instance, Marvin George, a member of Arts in Action, explained to me in an interview how they tried to investigate themes and subjects by dealing with a variety of social problems through the lens of theatre. The Arts in Action collaborative performances are aimed to promote the performing arts as a means to changing social perspectives and promoting social development by using characters from the folk or carnival traditions.

The object of their representations is the oppressed and the border-line situations; thereby, as marginalized object of the Caribbean society, women and their realities are also a frequent theme of their representations. For example their seminal work, »Dolly Mois A Cry Against Violence« (1994) was a constructive response to the high frequency with which reports of battered women and instances of domestic violence had reached the news headlines; the demonstration I saw during the Colloquium organized at the Centre for Creative and Festival Arts, St. Augustine Campus UWI, Trinidad, in 2006 was dealing with issues of parenting, exalting, through the use of the baby doll carnival mask, the common problematic of thousands of Caribbean mothers who are left alone by their partners, with the weight of family responsibilities weighing heavily on their shoulders. In this case, the baby doll mask has a cathartic function, rather than just aesthetic, which is finalized to pose important questions and honour to its audience by bringing them into an arena where they may discuss how violence might eventually be resolved.

On the 8th March 2006 the baby doll mask underwent a similar exercise, taken to the stage of the International Women's Day manifestation (public meeting campaign). Hazel Brown, president of the Network of NGOs of Trinidad and Tobago for the Advancement of Women, jumped on the stage with her costume, a version of the baby doll, in order to the new issues regarding birth control. A couple of days after, she explained to me that the use of carnival characters for the campaign is a powerful way to get through the media, to reach that kind of attention that has always been denied to women. In this process, traditional characters are individualized and symbolized, becoming themselves the impersonation of what their mask portrays; they are the subject of the representation- rather than just the lens through which the character is represented- who tells and acts, being, as in Carnival, the protagonist of the story.

The theatrical mimesis makes their story verisimilar, which means, that the characters do not tell us the chronicle about the past they represent, but about a present or a future that might be, echoing Turner's subjunctive mood of social drama. The reflexive catharsis that the audience feel is more like Pirandello's bitter laugh, rather than Aristotle's empathy, for they represent the modern allegory of the classic hero, echoing maybe a hybridized Don Quixote, rather then the tragic Oedipus. They are, in fact, the synthesis of the magical African folk traditions which encounter the almost lost western grotesque traditions of the fools, in a continuum process of transformation, hybridization (successively with other cultures too), and regeneration.

Carnival metalanguage and mimicry, whether unmasked on the road or masked on the stage, enable the »second sex« to destabilize the ideologized position and relation of power constructed on the unequal dichotomies, which were inhered from the colonial past. The relation between carnival and marginalization may be not only a place for visibility, but the space par excellence where women of all colours, ages, and classes are able to enact different forms of political and cultural activism, seeking for that equality that carnival promotes, representing the unique place where: »Only equals may laugh«.[201]

---

201 Bakhtin (1984): op. cit., p. 92

VII. CONCLUSION

> Old pirates, yes, they rob I;
> Sold I to the merchant ships,
> Minutes after they took I
> From the bottomless pit.
> But my hand was made strong
> By the 'and of the Almighty.
> We forward in this generation
> Triumphantly.
> Won't you help to sing
> These songs of freedom? -
> 'Cause all I ever have:
> Redemption songs;
> Redemption songs.
>
> Emancipate yourselves from mental slavery;
> None but ourselves can free our minds.
> [...]
>
> How long shall they kill our prophets,
> While we stand aside and look? Ooh!
> Some say it's just a part of it:
> We've got to fulfil de book...
> (Bob Marley, Redemption Song)

Trinidad carnival is the contextualised paroxysm of the society by which it is generated; it is the *mise en scène* of the starling ability of human beings to create themselves, to transform and renew, acting out and celebrating the contradictions experienced by the collectivity, and, at the same time, objectifying alternative possibilities that might replace the *status quo*.

Richard Schechner calls carnival- like events »direct theatre«, that is, the first theatre, raw materials for a new-universally second theatre, which »is carnivalesque in that the struggle—at certain key moments—is an exposure of what is wrong with the way things are and an acting out of the desired hoped-for new social relations. [...] Events are synecdochic and transparent: issues are debated, symbols paraded, agonists put square in the public eye. People...have to decide which side to be on.«[202] Thus, carnival is the ritual like activity that allows the hyperbolic display of social relations, transforming large public spaces into theatres, where collective reflexivity is performed, fecund and spectacular excesses displayed, by repositioning itself in places where the public life and social ritual have traditionally been acted out.

Carnival is a place where culture could articulate the image of itself and its self-understanding, displaying this image before its own members and members of other cultures, by providing the community with an awareness of Self and in this sense, a self-consciousness -whether as member of a culture, a nation, an ethnic group, a religious community, a social class or group, a family, or as an individual. In different cultures and epochs, carnival realises this general condition in very different and specific ways, raising always a question of (in structural terms) the creation of identity and changing identities, becoming itself the past, present, and future narrative of the community itself.

The masks and voices of carnival resist, exaggerate, and destabilize the distinctions and boundaries that mark and maintain high culture and organized society. But, by discourse, masks and disguises, by cloaking protest and criticism in the temporary topsy-turvy carnival laughter, it also reveals and discloses, giving voice and »recentralizing« the subarlterns, located normally at the margins. Its effect is to destabilize the normative distinctions and dichotomies, deconstructing the conventional ideologies that aliment them, by remapping social categories and »refashioning« social identities, whilst giving active voice to the »hidden« subalterns that are otherwise repressed. Therefore the unruly woman and her increasing presence in the contemporary Trinidad carnival is partly a chance for temporary release from the traditional and stable hierarchy; but it is also part of the conflict over efforts to change the basic distribution of power within society.

The carnivalized woman embodies the most despised aspects of »strong« femininity, and her subordinate position in society is in part underlined in this enactment of power rever-

---

202 Schechner (1993): op. cit., p. 88

sal. Femininity becomes the mask which displays the ambiguity and contradictions between the daily roles played by Caribbean women, and the ones they are expected to play within the societal normative structure, unmasking the power relations that are being almost simultaneously affirmed and denied.

Sexualized Caribbean bodies come forward in Caribbean carnival as self-actualizing and transformative, as sexual agents that shape and are shaped by larger political and economic forces, social structures and institutions, and relations of ethnicity and gender. The interplay between macro- and micro-forces, to which Caribbean society is constantly exposed, produces new conflicts, impulses, and dynamics of social change. Common everyday understandings of gender relations, and the collective strategies arise from the complexities and contradictions embedded in imagining women as a historical and ideological social construction, or, better to say, in how discourse has created the category of »woman« and what is at stake -politically, economically, and socially- in maintaining or dismissing that category.

Carnival is an empowering mimetic and absurd representation that begs for questioning, whose object is extended beyond the racial politics, aiming to confront the problematic of sexual constructions within Caribbean society.

The Caribbean »woman is boss« (Denis Plummer's calypso) may be interpreted as the allegoric representation of the strong-exotic black Matriarch, that is, the ideological emasculation and simultaneous objectification of Caribbean women resulting from a industrializing manoeuvre aiming at a new economical upturn in the name of global capitalism, with the internal consequences of new societal assets, that is, for instance, the decrease of male labour's demands and the following increase of the number of women in the educational and labour systems. In fact, according to Eudine Barriteau:

> »This had led to superficial analysis and irrelevant policies. The state ignores the contradictions between prioritizing the values of consumerism and mass consumption advocated by the modernization paradigm, and the increasing pauperization and subordination of many women. [...] Ideological relations of gender are at their worst for Caribbean women: women now exist in a climate of hostile gender relation. This

hostility is fed by men and women who argue that the Caribbean feminist movement exists to emasculate and marginalize men. [...] With the adverse economic climate of the last decade, some men have taken out their frustration on women. Several men admit to feel hostile to and threatened by women whom they perceive to be gaining material and psychological advantages over them.«[203]

Thus, especially in the Caribbean, past socializations have different impacts on the present; in fact, while independence was achieved, changes were and still are difficult to effect, for Caribbean people have internalized their past, reproducing stereotypes, expectations, and responses to others and to themselves. That is to say that the paradoxes and contradictions of gender relations in the Caribbean are alimented by both women and men; women by believing the stereotypes applied to them, and men by believing and perpetuating the own stereotypes about women.

While women's position in carnival evolves and changes, and while in other spheres of activities, in the household and in the community, women have demonstrated considerable leadership qualities, there are still threads of continuity reflecting women traditional roles and their relationships with men, and the general tendencies worldwide for a low proportion of women to be involved in the economic and political decision making. Therefore, the process directed at empowering women might focus on the values system, addressing the ideological issues that, in the Caribbean, have always been patriarchal and exclusionary of women's interests in public domain, while stressing the fact that women empowerment is not a synonymous with men disempowerment, but, on the contrary, the first step to equality.

Because of the Caribbean colonial past, its present and hybrid national configuration , and for the Caribbean/black female body was and still is the contested site, that is, the battleground for competing ideologies constructed through colonial and post-colonial (and by this time it might be referred also to

---

[203] Barriteau Eudine (1998): »Theorizing Gender Systems and the Project of Modernity in the Twentieth-Century Caribbean«, Femminist Review No 59, Summer 1998, p. 204

neo colonial) discourses and practices, Carnival, with its »time–defined/flexible –open« and »conformist/revolutionary« »anti-structure«, creates a dialogue among some of the major issues (language, commodification, sexuality, and performance) that affect the Caribbean, both on local and global level.

The dialogic laughter, with its ludic double negatives, becomes the conflictual and critical laughter of social subjects in any contemporary classic, racist, and sexist society, where women can overcome ideological barriers, by shaping the spectacle to conform to their own desire, once they learn its rules. Thus, Trinidad Carnival will always renew and recreate itself, remaining forever on the horizon with a continuum of new social subjectivity.

REFERENCES

Aching, Gerard (2002): »Masking and Power, Carnival and Popular Culture in the Caribbean«, University of Minnesota Press, Minneapolis, London.
Albertazzi, Silvia (2000): »Lo Sguardo dell'Altro«, Carrocci Editrice, Roma.
Alexander, Bobby, C. (1991): »Victor, Turner Revisited, Ritual as Social Change«, The American Academy of Religion, Scholar Press, Atlanta, Georgia.
Amadiume, Ifi (1987): »Male Daughters, Female Husbands: Gender and Sex in an African Society«, Zed Books, New York.
Amadiume, Ifi (1997): »Re-Inventing Africa: Matriarchy, Religion, and Culture«, Zed Books, London, New York.
Anderson, Benedict (1991) [1983]: »Imagined Communities Reflection on the Origin and Spread of Nationalism«, Verso, London; New York.
Aristotele (2001³): »Poetica«, Traduzione e Introduzione di Guido Padano, Editori Laterza, Bari, Roma.
Ashcroft, Bill (2001): »On Post-Colonial Futures, Transformation of Colonial Culture«, The Tower Building, London.
Aschcroft, Bill/Garreth, Griffiths/Tiffin, Helen (1994) [1989]: »The Empire Writes Back, Theory and Practice in Postcolonial Literature«, Routledge, New York and London.
Aschcroft, Bill/Garreth, Griffiths/Tiffin, Helen (1998): »Key Concepts in Post-Colonial Studies«, Routledge, New York and London.
Aschcroft, Bill/Garreth, Griffiths/Tiffin, Helen (2004) [1995]: »The Postcolonial Studies Reader«, Routledge, New York and London.
Awolalu, Omosade, J. (1979): »Yoruba Beliefs and Sacrificial Rites«, Longman Group Limited, London.

Babcock, Barbara, A. (edited by) (1978): »The Reversible World, Symbolic Inversion in Art and Society«, Cornell University Press, Ithaca and London.

Bakhtin, Mikhail, M (1981): »The dialogic Imagination, Four Essays«, University of Texas Press, Austin.

Bakhtin, Mikhail, M (1984): »Rabelais and His World«, Indiana University Press, Bloomington and Indianapolis.

Bailey, Barbara/Leo-Rhynie, Elsa (2004): »Gender in the 21st Century, Caribbean Perspectives, Visions and Possibilities«, Ian Randle Publishers, Kingston.

Balme, B., C. (1999): »Decolonizing the Stage, Theatrical Syncretism and Post-Colonial Drama«, Clarendon Press, Oxford.

Barnard, Alan/Spencer, Jonathan (edited by) (2002): »Encyclopaedia of Social and Cultural Anthropology«, Routledge, New York and London.

Barriteau, Eudine (1998): »Theorizing Gender Systems and the Project of Modernity in the Twentieth-Century Caribbean«, Femminist Review No 59, Summer 1998.

Barriteau, Eudine (2001): »The Political Economy of Gender in the Twentieth-Century Caribbean«, Palgrave, New York.

Barriteau, Eudine (edited by) (2003): »Theorizing Gender: Interdisciplinary Perspectives in the Caribbean«, University Press of the West Indies, Kingston, Jamaica.

Barrow, Christine (edited by) (1998): »Caribbean Portraits ‚Essays on Gender Ideologies and Identities«, Ian Randle Publishers, Kingston.

Bastide, Roger (1971): »African Civilisation in the New World«, C. Hurst & Company, London.

Bell, Catherine (1992): »Ritual Theory, Ritual Practice«, Oxford University Press, New York, Oxford.

Bell, Catherine (1997): »Ritual, Perspectives and Dimensions«, Oxford University Press, New York, Oxford.

Berrian, Brenda (1994): »Claming an Identity, Caribbean Women Writers in English, in Journal of Black Studies«, Vol. 25, No.2 (Dec., 1994), Sage Publications, pp. 200-216.

Best, Curwen (2001): »Roots to Popular Culture, Aesthetics: Kamau Brathwaite to Hardcore Styles«, Macmillan Education Ltd, London, Oxford.

Bhabha, Homi, K. (1990): »Nation and Narration«, Routledge, New York and London.

Bhabha, Homi, K. (1994): »The Location of Culture«, Routledge, New York and London.
Billig, Michael (2005): »Laughter and Ridicule«, Sage Publications, London.
Blake, F.I.R. (1995): »The Trinidad and Tobago Steel Pan, History and Evolution«, printed in Spain by Graphiques, Library of Congress cataloguing publication data.
Boehmer, Elleke (1995): »Colonial and Postcolonial Literature, Migrant Metaphors«, Oxford University Press, Oxford.
Brathwaite, Kamau (1990): »Alarms of God- Konnu and Carnival in the Caribbean«, in Caribbean Quarterly: »Konnu and Carnival-Caribbean Festival Arts«, vol. 36, nos. 3&4, special issue, University of the West Indies, Kingston, Jamaica.
Brereton, Bridget (1975): »The Trinidad Carnival 1870-1900«, Savacou 11-12, Sept 1975, edited by the Caribbean Artists Movement, Herald Ltd, Kingston, Jamaica.
Brereton, Bridget/Yelvington, Kevin, A.(edited by) (1999): »The Colonial Caribbean in Transition, Essays on Postemancipation Social and Cultural History«, The Press University of the West Indies, Kingston, Jamaica.
Bristol, Michael, D. (1985): »Carnival and Theatre, Plebeian Culture and the Structure of Authority in Renaissance England«, Methuen, New York and London.
Brydon, Lynne/Sylvia Chant (1989): »Women in the Third World, Gender Issues in Rural and Urban Areas«, Edward Elgar Publishing Limited.
Bulbeck, Chilla (1998): »Re-orienting Western Feminism, Women's Diversity in a Postcolonial World«, Cambridge University Press, Cambridge.
Burke, Peter (1997): »Varieties of Cultural History«, Cornell University Press, Ithaca, New York.
Burton, D., E., Richard (1997ce): »Afro-Creole, Power, Opposition, and Play in the Caribbean«, Cornell University Press, Ithaca, London.
Butler, Judith (1999): »Gender Trouble, Feminism and Subversion of Identity«, Routledge, New York and London.
Cain, E., William (2001): »Literary Criticism and Cultural Theory«, Garland Publishing, New York, London.
Calvino, Italo (1993): »Le città invisibili«, Mondadori, Milano.
Calvino, Italo (1997): »Invisible Cities«, Vintage, London.

Campbell, Carl/Higman, B., W./Moore Brian L. (edited by) (2001): »Slavery, Freedom and Gender: The Dynamics of Caribbean Society«, University of the West Indies Press, Barbados.

Capone, Giovanna (1993): »Percorsi Immaginati«, Il Ventaglio, Bologna.

Caribbean Quarterly (2000): »Carnival Monograph«, Kingston, Jamaica.

Caribbean Quarterly: »Calypso Monograph«, Kingston, Jamaica.

Caro, Baroja, Julio (1979): »El Carnaval, Análiasis Histórico-Cultural«, Taurus, Madrid.

Césaire, Aimé (1955): »Discourse sur le Colonialism«, Presence Africaine, Paris.

Césaire, Aimé (2000): »A Tempest«, based on Shakeskpeare's The tempest : adaptation for a black theatre, tr. Crispin Philip, Oberon, London.

Childs, Peter/Williams Patick R. J.(1997): »An Introduction to Post-Colonial Theory«, Prentice-Hall, London.

Cohen, Abner (1993): »Masquerade Politics, Exploration in the Structure of Urban Cultural Movement«, Berg Publisher Limited, Oxford, Providence.

Cohen, Ballerino, Colleen/Wilk, Richard/Stoeltje, Beverly (1996): »Beauty Queens on the Global Stage, Routledge«, New York and London.

Cooper, Carolyn (1995): »Noises in the Blood, Orality, Gender, and the 'Vulgar' Body of Jamaican Popular Culture«, Duke University Press, Durham.

Coquery-Vidrovitch (1997): Catherine: »African Women, A Modern History«, Westview Press, Oxford.

Crowley, Daniel ,J. (1988): »The Carnival of Guinea Bissau«, TDR, Vol.33 No. 2 (Summer1989).

Cowley, John (1996): »Carnival, Canboulay and Calypso, Traditions in the Making«, Cambridge University Press, Cambridge.

Cudjoe, Selwyn, R. (2003): »Beyond Boundaries: The Intellectual Tradition of Trinidad and Tobago in the Nineteenth Century«, Calaloux Publications, Wellesley.

Cudjoe, Selwyn, R. (1990): »Caribbean Women Writers, Essays from the First International Conference«, Calaloux Publications, Wellesley.

Daniel, Yvonne (2005): »Dancing Wisdom, Embodied Knowledge in Haitian Vodou, Cuban Yoruba, and Bahian Candomblé«, Sophia Smith of Smith College, United States of America.

Davis, Zemon, Natalie (1975): »Society and Culture in Early Modern France«, Gerald Duckworth Company Limited, London.

De Freitas, Patricia, A. (1999): »Disrupting the Nation: Gender and Transformations in the Trinidad Carnival«, New West Indian Guide/Nieuwe West-Indische Gids, 73 1 et 2, KITLV, Leiden, the Netherlands.

Diamond, Elin (edited by) (1996): »Performance and Cultural Politics«, Routledge, New York and London.

Drewal, Henry, John/Drewal, Thompson, Margaret (1990) [1983]: »Gélédè, Art and female Power among the Yoruba«, Indiana University Press, Bloomington, Indianapolis.

Drewal, Thompson, Margaret (1992): »Yoruba Ritual, Performers, Play, Agency«, Indiana University Press, Bloomington, Indianapolis.

Dudley, Shannon (2004): »Carnival Music in Trinidad«, Oxford University Press, New York, Oxford.

Durkheim, Emile (1995): »The Elementary Forms of Religious Life«, New York, The free Press, New York.

Eco, Umberto/Ivanov, V., V./Rector, Monica (1984): »Carnival!, Approaches to Semiotics«, edited by Thomas A. Sebeok, Mouton, Berlin, New York.

Eibl-Eibesfeldt, Irenäus (1997): »Die Biologie menschlichen Verhaltens. Grundriss der Humanethologie«, Piper, München.

Elder, J.,D. (1988): »African Survivals«, Karia Press, London.

Elder, J.,D (1998): »Cannes Brulees«, TDR, vol.42 No.3, Trinidad and Tobago Carnival (Autumn, 1998).

Eliade, Mircea (1959[2]): »The Sacred and the Profane, The Nature of Religion«, Harvest/HBJ book, New York and London.

Eliade, Mircea (1972): »Shamanism, Archaic Techniques of Ecstasy« Princeton University Press, Princeton, Oxford.

Eliade, Mircea (1993): »Enciclopedia delle religioni«, Marzorati, Milano.

Eliade, Mircea (1995²): »Rites and Symbols of Initiation, The Mysteries of Birth and Rebirth«, Spring Pubblications Inc., Woodstock.

Ellis,Pat (1986): »Women of the Caribbean«, Zed Books Ltd, London & New Jersey.

Etter-Lewis, Gwendolyn/Foster, Michéle (1996): »Unrelated Kin: Race and Gender in Women's Personal Narratives«, Routledge, New York and London.

Euba, Achin (1990): »Yoruba Drumming, Lagos, Electro Music Centre«, University of Lagos, Eckhard Breitinger University of Bayreuth, Bayreuth.

Euripide (1989): »Baccanti«, traduzione di Guidorizzi Giulio, Marsilio, Venezia.

Falola, Toyin/ Matt, D., Childs (edited by) (2004): »The Yoruba Diaspora in the Atlantic World«, Indiana University Press, Bloomington and Indianapolis.

Falola, Toyin/ Genova, Ann (edited by) (2005): »Yoruba Creativity, Fiction, Language, Life and Songs«, Africa World Press, Trenton, Asmara.

Fanon, Frantz (1967): »The Wretched of the Earth«, Penguin Books, Harmondsworth, Middlesex England.

Fanon, Frantz (1986) [1967]: »Black Skin, White Masks«, Pluto Press, London.

Fedre, Ellen, K./ Rawlinson, Mary, C./ Zakin, Emily (edited by) (1997): »Derrida and Feminism, Recasting the Question of Woman«, Routledge, New York and London.

Fierher, M. Thomas/ Lodwick, Michael, W. (edited by) (1990) [1979]: »Plantation Society in the Americas- Carnival in Perspective, An Interdisciplinary Journal of Tropical and Subtropical History and Culture«, Popular Press, Bowling Green, Ohio.

Fontenrose, Joseph 1974 [1959]: »Python, A Study of Delphic Myth and Its Origins«, Biblo-Tannen., New York.

Foote, Russell (2005): »Carnival: Contemporary Cruciale of the Social Sciences«, School of Continuing Studies UWI, St. Augustine, Trinidad.

Forde, Daryll (1951): »The Yoruba speaking peoples of South Western Nigeria«, in Ethnographic Survey of Africa part IV, International African Institute, London.

Forbes, Curdella (2005): »From nation to Diaspora, Samuel Selvon, George Lamming and the Cultural Performance of Gender«, The University of West Indies Press, Mona Kingston, Jamaica.

Frazer, James, George, Sir (1920): »The Golden Bough, a study in magic and religion«, Macmillan, & Co, London.

Gaino, Elle, J.(edited by) (1995): »Imperialism and Theatre, Essays on World Theatre, Drama and Performance«, Routledge, New York and London.

Galbiati, Gilberto (2003): »Le figlie di Pandora, la Donna, le Vere Ragioni della sua Millenaria Schiavitù«, Firenze Atheneheum, Firenze.

Gandhi, Leela (1998): »Postcolonial Theory, A Critical Introduction«, Edinburgh University Press, Edinburgh.

Gellner, Ernest (1983): »Nations and Nationalism«, Blackwell, Oxford, Basil.

Genovese, Eugene, D.(1976): »Roll, Jordan, Roll, the World the Slaves Made«, Vintage Books Edition, Usa.

Gernet Louis, Antropologia della Grecia Antica, Milano, Mondadori, 1982.

Geertz Clifford (2000) [1973]: »The Interpretation of Cultures«, New York, Basic Books.

Gherardi, Silvia (1995): »Gender, Symbolism and Organizational Cultures«, SAGE Publications Inc, London.

Gilbert, Helen (2001): »Postcolonial Plays, An Anthology«, Routledge, New York and London.

Gilbert, Helen/Tompkins, Joanne (1996): »Post-Colonial Drama, Theory, Practice, Politics«, Routledge, New York and London.

Gilmore, David (1995): »The Scholar Minstrels of Andalusia: Deep Oratory, or the Carnivalesque Upside Down«, Journal of the Royal Anthropological Institute, Vol. 1, No.3, Sep.1995, pp.561-580.

Gilmore, David (1998): »Carnival and Culture: Sex, Symbol, and Status in Spain«, Yale University Press, New Haven, Conn, London.

Gilroy, Paul (1993): »The Black Atlantic, Modernity and Double Consciousness«, Verso, London, New York.

Gnisci, Armando/Sinopoli, Franca, (1995): »Comparare i Comparatismi«, Lithos Editrice, Roma.

Goddard, Victoria, Ana (2000): »Gender, Agency, and Change: Anthropological Perspectives«, Routledge, New York and London.

Goff, Barbara (2004): »Citizen Bacchae, Women's Ritual Practice in Ancient Greece«, University of California Press, Berkley.

Golden, Mark/ Toohey, Peter (edited by) (2003): »Sex and Difference in Ancient Greece and Rome«, Edinburgh University Press, Edinburgh.

Gowricharn, Ruben (edited by) (2006): »Caribbean Transnationalism, Migration, Pluralisation, and Social Cohesion«, Lexington Books, Oxford.

Grant,Trevor, L. (2004): »Carnivalitis«, Yacos Publications, New York.

Green, Garth, L./ Scher, Philip, W. (edited by) (2007): »Trinidad Carnival, the Cultural Politics of a Transnational Festival«, Indiana University Press, Bloomington, Indianapolis.

Harding, Frances (edited by) (2002): »The Performances in Africa«, Routledge, New York and London.

Harris, Max (1998): »The Impotence of Dragons: Playing Devil in Trinidad Carnival«, TDR (1988), Vol.42 No.3, (Autumn 1998), 108-123.

Harrison, Carter, Paul/Walker, Victor, Leo II/Edwards Gus (edited by) (2002): »Black Theatre, Ritual Performance in the African Diaspora«, Temple University Press, Philadelphia.

Herskovits, Melville, J. (1958): »The Myth of the Negro Past«, Beacon Press, Boston.

Hill, Errol (edited by) (1963): »The artists in West Indian Society, a Symposium«, Department of Extra-Mural Studies, University of West Indies.

Hill, Errol (1997) [1972]: »The Trinidad Carnival: Mandate for a National Theatre«, University of Texas, Austin.

Hollis, »Chalkdust«, Liverpoool (1998): »Origins of Rituals and Customs in the Trinidad Carnival: African or European?«, TDR Vol. 42, No.3, Trinidad and Tobago Carnival, (August 1998), pp. 24-37.

Hollis, »Chalkdust«, Liverpoool (2001): »Rituals of Power and Rebellion, The Carnival Tradition in Trinidad and Tobago— 1763-1962«, Research Associated School Times, Publications Frontline Distribution Int'l Inc., Chicago, Jamaica, London, republic of Trinidad and Tobago.

Hobsbawm, Eric/Ranger Terence (1983): »The Invention of Tradition«, Cambridge University Press, Cambridge.

Hoch-Smith, Judith/ Spring, Anita (1978): »Women in Ritual and Symbolic Roles«, Plenum Press, New York & London.

Hofstadter, Albert/Kuhns Richard (edited by) (1976) [1964]: »Philosophies of Art and Beauty, Selected Reading in Aesthetics from Plato to Heidegger«, The University of Chicago Press, Chicago.

Holquist, Michael (1992): »Bakhtin and Rabelais: Theory as Praxis«, in Boundary 2, Vol.11, No.1/2 (Autumn, 1992- Winter, 1983), Duke University Press, pp. 5-19.

Honore, Brian (1998): »The Midnight Robber: Master of Metaphor, Baron of Bombast« TDR (1988), Vol.42 No.3, Trinidad and Tobago Carnival, (Autumn, 1998), pp. 124-131

Hooks, Bell (1990): »Yearning: Race, Gender and Cultural Politics«, South End Press, Boston.

Hutchinson, John/Smith, Antony, D. (edited by) (1994): »Nationalism«, Oxford University Press, Oxford, New York.

James, Joy/Sharpley-Whiting, Denan, T. (2000): »The Black Feminist Reader«, Blackwell Publishers, Oxford.

Jeanmaire, Henri (1972): »Dioniso: Religione e Cultura«, Einaudi, Torino.

Johnson, Allan, G. 2005 [1997]: »The Gender Knot, Unravelling Our Patriarchal Legacy«, Temple, United States of America.

Johnson, Kim/Gay, Derek (1998): »Notes on Pan«, TDR (1988), Vol.42 No.3, Trinidad and Tobago Carnival (Autumn 1998), pp. 61-73.

Jung, Carl, Gustav (1978): »Man and his Symbols«, Pan Books, London.

Jung, Carl, Gustav/Kerény, Károly 2003 [1972]: »Prolegomeni allo Studio Scientifico della Mitologia«, tr. Berlich, Angelo, Universale Bollati Boringhieri, Torino.

Keuls, Eva, C. 1993 [1985]: »The Reign of the Phallus, Sexual Politics in Ancient Athens, Berkeley«, University of California Press, London, Los Angeles.

Kincaid, Jamaica (1988): »A Small Place«, Penguin Books, London.
Knapp, Bettina L. (1987): »Women in Twentieth-Century Literature: A Jungian View«, University Press, University Park, Pennsylvania State.
Koningsbruggen van, Peter (1997): »Trinidad Carnival, A Quest for National Identity«, Mcmillan Education Ltd, London, Basingstoke.
Lancaster, Roger, N. (1997): »Leonardo di Micaela, The Gender Sexuality Reader, Culture, History, Political Economy«, Routledge, New York and London.
Littlefield, Kasfir, Sidney (1998): »Elephant Women, Furious and Majestic, Women's Masquerades in Africa and Diaspora, African Arts«, Spring 1998, UCL James S.Coleman African Studies Center, pp. 18-27.
Lombardo, Agostino (1995): »Le orme di Prospero«, La Nuova Italia Scientifica, Roma.
Loomba, Ania (1998): »Colonialism/Postcolonialism«, Routledge, London and New York.
Lovelace, Earl (1998) [1979]: »The Dragon Can't Dance«, Faber and Faber, London, Boston.
Lovelace, Earl (1998): »The Emancipation-Jouvay Tradition and the Almost Loss of the Pan«, TDR (1998), Vol.42 No.3, Trinidad and Tobago Carnival (Autumn 1998), pp. 54-60.
Mason, Peter (1998): »Bacchanal! The Carnival Culture in Trinidad«, Temple University Press, Philadelphia.
Magali, Cornier, Michael (1996): »Feminism and the Postmodern Impulse«, State University of New York Press, Albany.
Martin, Carol (1998): »Trinidad Carnival Glossary«, (TDR 1988) Vol. 42 No.3, Trinidad and Tobago Carnival (Autumn 1998), pp. 220-235.
Mauss, Marcel (2001) [1972]: »A General Theory of Magic«, Routledge, NewYork and London.
McAuslan, Ian/Walcot Peter (1996): »Women in Antiquity«, Oxford University Press, Oxford.
Mead, Margaret (1970) [1967]: »Male and Female, A Study of the Sexes in a Changing World«, William Morrow & Company, New York.
Miller, Daniel (1991): »Absolute Freedom in Trinidad«, in Man, New Series, Vol. 26, No.2 (Jun.,1991), 323-341, Royal An-

thropological Institute of Great Britain and Irland, pp. 323-341.
Mintz, Sidney, W.: »Social stratification and cultural pluralism«, in Horowitz, Michael, M.(edited by) (1971): »Peoples and culture of the Caribbean, An Anthropological Reader«, The Natural History Press, Garden City, New York.
Mintz, Sidney, W./Price, Sally (edited by) (1985): »Caribbean Contours«, The Johns Hopkins University Press, Baltimore, London.
Mintz, Sidney, W. (1989): »Caribbean Transformations«, Columbia University Press, New York.
Mohammed, Patricia (edited by) (2002): »Gendered Realities: Essays in Caribbean Feminist Thought«, University of the West Indies Press, Barbados.
Mohammed, Patricia/Shepherd Catherine (edited by) (1999): »Gender and Caribbean Development«, Canoe Press, University of West Indies, Kingston.
Moore-Gilbert Bart (1997): »Postcolonial Theory, Contexts, Practices, Politics«, Verso, London.
Moore, Henrietta, L. (1988): »Feminism and Anthropology«, Polity Press, Cambridge.
Murray, David, A., B. (2002): »Opacity, Gender, Sexuality, Race, and the 'Problem' of Identity in Martinique«, Peter Lang, New York.
Newson, Adele, S./Strong-Leek, Linda (1998): »Winds of Change: The Transforming Voices of Caribbean Women Writers and Scholars«, Peter Lang, New York.
Ngũgĩ, wa, Thiong'o, (1997): »Enactments of Power: The politics of Performance Space«, TDR 1988, Vol. 41 No.3, (Autumn 1997), The MIT Press, pp. 11-30.
Nunley, John (1988): »Purity and Pollution in Freetown: Masked Performance« (TDR 1988), Vol. 32, No. 2 (Summer, 1988), pp. 102-122.
Nunley, John, W./Bettelheim, Judith/Bridges, Barbara, A. (1988): »Caribbean Festival Arts: Each and Every Bit of Difference«, University of Washington Press, Seattle.
Nurse, Keith/ Ho, G.T, Christine (2005): »Globalisation, Diaspora and Caribbean Popular Culture«, National Library of Jamaica Cataloguing in Publication Data, Kingston.

Okediji, Qladejo, O. (1970): »The Sociology of the Yoruba«, Ibadan University Press, Ibadan.

Parkin, David, J./Caplan, Lionel/Fisher, Humphrey, J. (edited by) (1996): »The Politics of Cultural Performance«, Berghahn Books, Providence, Oxford.

Patel, Sampat (2001): »Postcolonial Masquerades, Culture and Politics in Literature, Film, Video, and Photography (Literary Criticism and Cultural Theory: the Interaction of Text and Society)«, Garland Publishing Inc., New York., London.

Pearse, Andrew (c1988) [1956]: »Carnival in Nineteenth Century Trinidad, Caribbean«, in Caribbean Quarterly, Trinidad Carnival, Trinidad Carnival Issue, Vol.4 Nos 3&4, Paria, Port of Spain, Trinidad.

Petersen, Kristen, Holst/Rutherford Anna (1986): »A Double Colonization, Colonial and Post-colonial Women's Writing«, Dangaroo Press, Oxford.

Pollock, Donald (1995) »Masks and the Semiotics of Identity«, The Journal of The Royal Anthropological Institute, Vol.1 No.3, (Sept. 1995), pp.581-597

Premdas, Ralph, R. (edited by) (2006): »Identity, Ethnicity and Culture in the Caribbean«, Trinidad, School of Continuing Studies, University of West Indies, St. Augustine.

Puri, Shalini (2004): »The Caribbean Postcolonial: Social Equality, Post-Nationalism, and Cultural Hybridity«, Palgrave Macmillan, New York, Basingstoke.

Quayson, Ato (2000): »Postcolonialism, Theory, Practice or Process?«, Polity Press, Cambridge.

Quevedo, Raymond (1994): »Attilla's Kaiso«, University of West Indies, School of Continuing Studies, St. Augustine, Trinidad.

Rang, F., C (1974): »Psicologia Storica del Carnevale«, Arsenale Editrice, Venezia.

Rappaport, Roy, A.(1999): »Ritual and Religion in the Making of Humanity«, Cambridge University Press, Cambridge.

Reddock, Rhoda, E. (edited by) (1994): »Interrogating Caribbean Masculinities, Theoretical and Empirical Analysis«, University of the West Indies Press, Mona, Kingston.

Regis, Humphery (edited by) (2001): »Culture and Mass Communication in the Caribbean«, University Press of Florida, Gainesville.

Reif-Hüsler, Monika/Sedlak, Werner (edited by) (1999): »Borderlands, Negotiating Boundaries in Post-Colonial Writing«, Rodopi, Amsterdam.

Reiss, Timothy, J. (edited by) (2005): »Music, Writing and Cultural Unity in the Caribbean«, Africa World press Inc., Asmara.

Richards, Kenneth/Richards Laura (1990): »The Commedia dell'Arte, A Documentary History«, Blackwell Ltd, Oxford, Basil.

Riggio, Cozart, Milla (1998): »Introduction, Resistance and Identity: Carnival in Trinidad and Tobago«, TDR 1988, Vol.42, No.3, Trinidad and Tobago Carnival (Autumn 1998), pp. 6-23.

Riggio, Cozart, Milla (edited by) (2004): »Carnival, Culture in Action-The Trinidad Experience«, Routledge, New York, London.

Roesler, W./Zimmermann, B. (1991): »Carnevale e Utopia nella Grecia Antica«, Levante Editori, Bari.

Radford, Ruether, Rosmary (edited by) (1974): »Religion and Sexism, Images of Woman in the Jewish and Christian Traditions«, Simon and Schuster, New York.

Rohlehr, Gordon (1990): »Calypso and Society in Preindependent Trinidad«, Lexicon Trinidad Ltd, Port of Spain.

Rohlehr, Gordon (1998): » 'We Getting the Kaiso That We Deserve': Calypso and the World Music Market«, Drama Revue 42, no. 3, pp. 82-95.

Rohlehr, Gordon (2004): »A Scuffling of Islands: Esseys on Calypso«, Lexicon Trinidad Ltd, San Juan.

Russo, Mary, J.(1995) [1994]: »The Female Grotesque: Risk, Excess, and Modernity«, Routledge, New York and London.

Sampietro, Luigi (edited by) (1991): »Caribana«, Vol. 2, Bulzoni Editore, Roma.

Said, Edward, W.(1991): »Orientalism«, Penguin, Harmondworth.

Said, Edward, W.(1993): »Culture and Imperialism«, Chatto and Windus, London.

Sausurre, Ferdinand, De (1974): »Course in General Linguistics«, Fontana, London.

Schechner, Richard (1988): »Performance Theory«, Routledge, New York and London.

Schechner, Richard (1993): »The Future of Ritual, Writings on Culture and Performance«, Routledge, New York and London.

Schechner, Richard (2002): »Performance Studies, An Introduction«, Routledge, New York and London.

Scher, Philip, W. (1999): »Confounding Categories: The Global and the Local in the Process of a Caribbean Art«, Small Axe: Caribbean Journal of Criticism Vol.: 3. Issue: 6, 1999, pp. 37-56.

Scher, Philip, W.(2003): »Carnival and the Formation of a Caribbean Transnation«, University Press of Florida, Gainesville.

Schwarz, Henry/Ray, Sangeeta (edited by) (2000), »A Companion to Postcolonial Studies, A Historical Introduction», Blackwell Publishers, Oxford.

Segal, Robert, A. (edited by) (1998): »The Myth and Ritual Theory, An Anthology«, Blackwell Publishers, Oxford.

Shepherd, Verene, A. (1999): »Women in Caribbean History«, Ian Randle Publishers, Kingston.

Shepherd, Verene/Richards, Glen, L. (edited by) (2002): »Questioning Creole, Creolisation Discourse in Caribbean Culture«, Ian Randle Publishers, Kingston.

Sistren/Ford-Smith, Honor (edited by) (1986): »Lionhaert Gal, Life Stories of Jamaican Women«, The Women's Press Limited, London.

Skeleton, Tracey (edited by) (2004): »Introduction to the Pan-Caribbean«, Hodder Arnold Headline Group, London.

Smith, Raymond, T. (1998): »The Matrifocal Family, Power, Pluralism, and Politics«, Routledge, New York and London.

Spivak, Gayatry, Chakravorty (1999) (2003 printing): »A Critique of Postcolonial Reason, Toward a History of the Vanishing Present«, Harvard University Press, Cambridge.

Stallybrass, Peter/White, Allon (1986): »The Politics and Poetics of Transgression«, Methuen & Co. Ltd, London.

Strauss, Lévi, Claude (1963): »Structural Anthropology«, Basic Books, New York.

Taylor, Patrick (edited by) (2001): »Nation Dance, Religion, Identity, and Cultural Difference in the Caribbean«, Indiana University Press, Bloomington.

Tessari, Roberto (1998): »La Drammaturgia da Eschilo a Goldoni«, Laterza, Roma, Bari.

Tessari, Roberto (2004): »Teatro e Antropologia: tra Rito e Spettacolo«, Carrocci, Roma.

Turner, Victor (1957): »Schism and Continuity in an African Society, A Study of Ndembu Village Life«, Manchester University Press, Manchester.

Turner, Victor (1967): »The Forest of Symbols: Aspects of Ndembu Ritual«; Cornell University Press, Ithaca (NY), London.

Turner, Victor (1969): »The Ritual Process, Structure and Anti/Structure«, Routledge & Kegan Paul, London.

Turner, Victor (1979): »Process, Performance and Pilgrimage«, Concept Publishing Company, New Delhi.

Turner, Victor (1975) [i.e.1976]: »Drama fields, and metaphors: symbolic action in human society«, Cornell University Press, Ithaca, London.

Turner, Victor (1979): »Frame Flow and Reflection, Ritual Drama as Public Liminality«, Japanese Journal of Religious Studies 4/6, pp. 465-499.

Turner, Victor (1982): »From Ritual to Theatre, The Human Seriousness of Play«, PAJ Publications, New York.

Turner, Victor (c1986): »The Anthropology of Performance«, PAJ Publications, New York.

Tucker, Robert, C. (edited by) (1978[2]): »The Marx-Engel Reader«, W.W Norton & Company, Princeton University.

Van Gennep, Arnold (1960): »The Rites of Passage«, London, Routledge and Kegan Paul, London.

Vincent, Joan (edited by) (2002): »The Anthropology of Politics, A Reader in Ethnography, Theory, and Critique«, Blackwell Publishing Ltd, Oxford.

Yelvington, Kevin, A. (1996): »Flirting in the Factory«, Journal of the Royal Anthropological Institute Institute of Great Britain and Irland, Vol. 2, pp. 313-333.

Young, Robert, J., C. (1995): »Colonial Desire, Hybridity in Theory, Culture and Race«, New York and London, Routledge.

Young, Robert, J., C (2001): »Postcolonialism. An Historical Introduction«, Blackwell Publishers, Oxford.

Warner-Lewis, Maureen (1991): »Guinea's Other Sun, The African Dynamic in Trinidad Culture«, The Majority Press, Dover.

Warner-Lewis, Maureen (1997): »Trinidad Yoruba«, The Press University of the West Indies, Kingston.

Warner-Lewis, Maureen (2003): »Central Africa in the Caribbean«, The Press University of the West Indies, Kingston.

Williams, Eric (1982^2): »History of the People of Trinidad and Tobago«, London, Andre Deutsch.

Williams, Patrick/Chrisman, Laura (edited and introduced by) (1994): »Colonial Discourse and Postcolonial Theory, A Reader«, Pearson Education Limited, Harlow.

Wilson, Peter, J. (1995) [1973]: »Crab Antics, A Caribbean Case Study of the Conflict Between Reputation and Respectability«, Waveland Press, Illinois.

ILLUSTRATIONS

Fig.1:   142
Fig.2:   143
Fig.3:   143
Fig.4:   144
Fig.5:   144
Fig.6:   145
Fig.7:   145
Fig.8:   146
Fig.9:   147
Fig.10:   148
Fig.11:   162
Fig.12:   164
Fig.13:   164
Fig.14:   165
Fig.15:   165
Fig.16:   166
Fig.17:   167
Fig.18:   167

Postcolonial Studies

SÉRGIO COSTA
Vom Nordatlantik zum »Black Atlantic«
Postkoloniale Konfigurationen und
Paradoxien transnationaler Politik

2007, 292 Seiten, kart., 28,80 €,
ISBN 978-3-89942-702-8

ANETTE DIETRICH
Weiße Weiblichkeiten
Konstruktionen von »Rasse« und
Geschlecht im deutschen Kolonialismus

2007, 430 Seiten, kart., 29,80 €,
ISBN 978-3-89942-807-0

KIEN NGHI HA
Unrein und vermischt
Postkoloniale Grenzgänge durch
die Kulturgeschichte der Hybridität
und der kolonialen »Rassenbastarde«

Mai 2010, 320 Seiten, kart., ca. 29,80 €,
ISBN 978-3-8376-1331-5

Leseproben, weitere Informationen und Bestellmöglichkeiten
finden Sie unter www.transcript-verlag.de